To Carol,
Co-creating u
@ The Center.

Wendy

WE THE PEOPLE
Consenting to a Deeper Democracy

A Guide to Sociocratic Principles and Methods

by John Buck and Sharon Villines

SOCIOCRACY.INFO

WASHINGTON DC

SOCIOCRACY.INFO
6827 Fourth Street NW #213
Washington, DC 20012

contact@sociocracy.info

Printed in the United States of America

First Edition, Second Printing with Corrections
ISBN: 978-0-9792827-0-6 (pbk)

We the People: Consenting to a Deeper Democracy, A Guide to Sociocratic Principles and Methods / by John Buck and Sharon Villines
p.   cm.

Includes illustrations, glossary, bibliography, index.

Buck, John
Villines, Sharon

Endenburg, Gerard
Boeke, Kees

1. Sociocracy. 2. Governance. 3. Dynamic governance. 4. Dynamic self-governance. 5. Cybernetics. 4. Systems thinking. 6. Corporate Governance.

Cover: Cotgrave Village, Nottinghamshire, UK.
Photo by Graham Heywood, grahamheywood.co.uk.

In Memory of Frank Ward,

Kees Boeke, and

Anna and Gerardus Endenburg

CONTENTS

APPENDICES: Additional Resources

LIST OF ILLUSTRATIONS

Illustrations 4.1, 5.1, 6.3, and 8.1 used with permission of the Sociocratisch Centrum; redrawn and digitized by Jason Forrest.

ABOUT THIS BOOK

Sociocracy, also known as dynamic governance or dynamic self-governance, is a method of organizing and governing ourselves using the principle of consent. How it produces more inclusive, sustainable, and productive organizations is the story of this book. It is also the story of how sociocracy promotes our society's most cherished values—equality, freedom, education, and entrepreneurial opportunity—more deeply than the forms of democracy that rule our civic lives or the autocratic structures that rule our work lives.

We the People is an introduction to sociocratic principles and methods, an exploration of the scientific theories on which they are based, and a manual for organizing sociocratically. In Part I, "Why Organize Sociocratically," we explain our personal reasons for believing that our society needs sociocracy and in Part II, "The Science of Sociocratic Governance," we explore the scientific principles behind its principles. Some readers will be interested in the whole story, start to finish, and others will want to jump right to the "how to" chapters in Part III, "How It Works." Wherever you start, we hope you will return to read the other chapters so you will fully understand this deeply enriching and effective method for getting more done, more harmoniously.

We appreciate the many people who have contributed to this book. We particularly thank Ramona Buck, Gerard Endenburg, and Greg Rouillard for their tireless proofing and detailed comments, and our many readers for their enthusiastic support of our work.

John Buck and Sharon Villines
November 2007

ABOUT THE AUTHORS

John Buck was the first native English-speaking consultant certified by the Sociocratisch Centrum in Rotterdam to teach and guide implementation of the sociocratic circle organization method. After he learned to read Dutch to gain full access to the literature and to study at the Sociocratisch Centrum, Buck has helped translate a number of key documents from the Dutch. With a BA from Brown University, he later completed an MA in Quantitative Sociology at George Washington University in order to measure the effects of sociocracy on Dutch workers. His thesis confirmed the effectiveness of the sociocratic method in increasing worker commitment to their companies.

Now CEO of Governance Alive, a consulting firm that specializes in new governance methods, Buck has extensive experience managing people in both government and corporate sectors. He runs workshops, consults, and serves on the boards of sociocratic organizations. He lives with his wife in Silver Spring, MD.

Sharon Villines, MFA, is a writer and artist and Mentor *Emeritus* at Empire State College, SUNY, where she mentored adult students in the arts, including arts management, and served on numerous governance committees. Also co-author of *Orientation to College: A Reader on Becoming an Educated Person* (Wadsworth, 2004), she now writes on a variety of topics related to community organization and governance, using her experience in nonprofit organizations, labor unions, universities, schools, religious and political action groups, cohousing, and other cooperative enterprises as a basis for helping others understand and apply sociocratic principles and methods. She lives in a cohousing community in Washington, DC.

PART I

Why Organize Sociocratically?

INTRODUCTION

Revisiting Governance

We the People of the United States, in Order to Form a More Perfect Union, establish Justice, insure domestic Tranquility, provide for the common defence, promote the general Welfare, and secure the Blessings of Liberty to ourselves and our Posterity, do ordain and establish this Constitution for the United States of America.

Sociocratic governance builds on the values and experience of democracy and the scientific discoveries of the twentieth century to create an even more participatory and inclusive system. The United States constitution created a government based on principles that had never been proven to work on a large scale, and its new governance structure was much more experimental than many of us realize. In addition, the founders of the United States were faced with uniting into one nation an unruly group of states that were exhausted from war, spoke many languages, and were still breaking links with their mother countries (Amar 2005).

Sociocracy is not quite so unproven and its advocates are not faced with these same challenges, but sociocracy is as potentially revolutionary—a peaceful revolution this time, conducted by consent, one that promises to be quiet, gradual, and nurturing.

Sociocracy derives its name from the Latin *socius*, "associates" or "companions." This is the same root used for *sociology*, the study of society, as well as for other words that refer to studies or attributes of social groups like *sociodynamic, socioecology, sociogram, sociometric,* and *socialist*. It is sometimes confused with socialism but socialism advocates central ownership and control of the means of production, capital, land, and property and functions by means of a central authority. While a socialist organization could, in theory, use sociocratic principles and methods, sociocracy does not advocate central ownership or control. On the contrary, it assumes a market economy and advocates "free organizations," owned by themselves.

Sociocracy is simply a method for organizing ourselves to live and work together more efficiently and more harmoniously. It can be used by one person, two persons, a corporation, a religious group, a neighborhood association, or a whole community to create more harmonious, more effective, and more productive ways of living and working together. One day, whole countries may use it.

Concerns over confusion with socialism, however, have led some sociocratic organizations to use other descriptors including "dynamic governance," "dynamic self-governance," "consent democracy," "direct democracy," and "circle governance." We've chosen to use *sociocracy*, *sociocratic governance*, and *sociocratic organizations* because these words are specific, less open to confusion, and link to the tradition of sociocratic thinking.

The principles of sociocracy are the same ones shared by most democratic societies, but we believe that sociocracy, because it provides a new organizational structure and a different basis for decision making, ensures what is only asserted in democracies, that all human beings are created equal and endowed by society with the undeniable rights of life, liberty, and the pursuit of happiness. Sociocracy ensures these principles will apply at all levels of an organization. Further, unlike democratic principles that are limited in practice to civic governments and voluntary organizations, sociocracy extends these principles to all organizations, including businesses.

Writing Our Own Constitutions

The title *We the People* was chosen deliberately because it is instantly recognizable as the opening phrase of the United States constitution. A constitution is a document written by people who consent to it to state the values and principles that will govern their lives together.

Sociocratic principles are designed to guide us in writing our own constitutions for our own organizations. A constitution is a set of policies that grants rights and privileges, sets limits on behavior, and assigns responsibilities. This means that all members of an organization—citizens, staff, managers, leaders, and investors—within their sphere of responsibility and within the over-all goals of the organization, can determine how they will accomplish their goals, how their work will be done and by whom, and what skills and resources they need to develop to remain competitive.

Sociocracy is simultaneously conservative and revolutionary. It encourages the productivity of a market economy and at the same time is deeply supportive of the ideals of individual freedom. A sociocratic organization ensures that the voices in the mail room and those in the board room are both heard.

The Discoveries of Science

Scientific discoveries in the twentieth century fundamentally altered our view of how the natural world works. The mechanical model of closed systems was superseded by the ever-changing and unpredictable world of open systems. Living organisms were discovered to be dynamic, self-correcting, and adjusting constantly to their environment. Even the adult brain, once thought to be steadily degrading until death, was discovered instead to be developing new neurons with each new challenge. Chaos was discovered to be not random or purposeless but potentially self-organizing and incredibly powerful and energetic.

Our organizations, however, are still based on the mechanical analogies of the nineteenth century and often treat people like machine parts, ignoring their abilities and their human potential. So how do we use our new understanding?

We the People is about how sociocracy takes what science has learned and applies it to create organizations as powerful, self-organizing, and self-correcting as the natural world.

Is It Practical?

Sociocracy is not only practical, it is easier. It works with nature instead of against it. It creates and directs energy, not just harnesses it. In the Netherlands in divisions of Shell, Heineken, Mars, and Pfizer, it has demonstrated that it is more productive. It is altering labor management relationships because it is less adversarial and provides better protection for workers' rights. In nationwide professional organizations, like the United States Green Building Council, it is respected for being efficient as well as egalitarian. In a small nursing home in Vermont, it is making a new holistic approach to elder care feasible.

Several Dutch university business schools now teach sociocracy and it is appearing more and more frequently on reading lists in American university courses in both business and sociology. The global circle with headquarters in the Sociocratisch Centrum, the international sociocratic association in Rotterdam, continues to develop sociocratic methods and applications.

In *We the People*, we introduce sociocracy and provide a handbook for implementation. In Part I, we present the history of sociocracy and the reasons why, based on our experience, we believe these principles and methods are so sensible and freeing. In Part II, we explain sociocratic concepts and methods and why they are effective. In Part III, we present the "how to", the procedures and techniques needed to transform your own organization into a sociocratically governed one.

The appendices include many documents that are unavailable elsewhere including historical texts, templates, and other sociocratic documents. The glossary of sociocratic terms following the appendices is extensive and includes many concepts that we were unable to fully explore in the text.

We also invite readers to connect with others who are learning about sociocracy and to share their experiences in applying the methods. There is more information on how to do this in the "Afterword: Next Steps."

CHAPTER ONE

Why We Need Another "–ocracy"

by John Buck

I encountered Gerard Endenburg and the sociocratic method more than twenty years ago while on a trip to Amsterdam to give a speech about computer-based training. I took my family, as well, and we had arranged a delightful stay with friends. One evening I vented to our host about my frustrations with the world of business.

"I am supposed to be living in a democracy," I said, "but I spend much of my life at work in a basically feudal structure. There is a Duke of Operations, an Earl of Administration, a Baroness of Personnel, and so on. Even if those people are called Managers or Vice-Presidents it amounts to the same thing. I am not at all enfranchised. If I think they aren't doing well, the only vote I have is with my feet walking out the door. I have done a lot of research in management literature, but I can't find anyone who has found a way to run an effective business democratically."

"Oh, but that problem has been solved," my host replied in her accented but impeccable English. "You must talk to Gerard Endenburg. He is the president of a very successful electrical engineering company. Let's call him up."

We were soon speeding on a solid Dutch train to Rotterdam to visit Gerard. My research had prepared me to probe in-depth in my talk with him, and in a short time, I was convinced that Gerard had indeed come up with something very rare: genuinely new and ingenious ideas about how to organize. He was not just tinkering with a different angle on worker participation. He had deep and practical insight into the fundamental nature of power. This book describes those insights. I have found that there is a real delight in using Gerard's new methods, and I have been enjoying bringing them to as many organizations as possible—businesses, schools, corporations, factories, associations, even to individuals.

How did I become so impassioned about having a job as an enfranchised citizen of a company rather than as an employee? And to want to share this possibility with others?

I am a baby boomer who, like all members of my generation, came of age to the sounds of anti-war protests and civil rights marches. I was not a radical. In fact, I handed out literature in favor of Barry Goldwater and was a runner up in my district for admittance to West Point. I opposed the Vietnam War not because I felt war was bad, but rather because I felt that particular war was an unconstitutional, presidential war. I received a safe number in the draft lottery and went to work in Seattle for Boeing as a technical writer, a conventional, proper thing to do with a liberal arts degree from an Ivy League university. More than the war, more than civil rights inequalities, it was my experience at Boeing that shocked awake in me a passion for trying to change the way my country and my society was functioning. As upsetting as the anti-war and civil rights demonstrations were, they were examples of a democracy in action, correcting itself—as it was designed to do. It involved tremendous citizen energy, but life at Boeing was a different matter.

Servitude

I was working for the Manufacturing Research and Development Division that had no union representation, but unions wouldn't have helped. All the unions could do was to negotiate the conditions of servitude. The term *public servant* is respectable, but not *private servant*, another name for an employee. I identified with the little boy who saw that the emperor had no clothes. I was a servant in a large room of about 200 other servants, all of us sitting in long rows of desks with phone cords hanging from the ceiling, enshrouded in a constant pall of cigarette smoke. Ironically, the cigarette smoke was the only personal gratification allowed in the room. Before we punched out each day we had to make sure our phones were on the back left corner of our desks so the room looked in perfect order.

My supervisor treated me well and I enjoyed my co-workers. Nothing overtly bad happened. I simply felt powerless, and something deep inside of me shredded.

I learned a lot at Boeing. I saw my first systems diagram—massive flow charts of the manufacturing process whose preparation was aided slightly by the massive mainframe computers then available. I learned that you needed to expect at least a 30-to-1 return before investing in a research and development project, and I saw long-term planning in operation one day when I peeked into a temporarily vacant executive conference room on "mahogany row." The chart on the wall predicted a gradual reduction in the number of airplane manufacturers over the next 25 years and listed recommendations for what Boeing had to do to survive those reductions, including the layoff that was about to sweep me away. The chart, it turned out, was very accurate. Boeing is now the last major airplane manufacturer in the United States.

I also learned that people could care incredibly. My first child was born the week before I was laid off. I was deeply touched when my co-worker, Jan, a woman of about 50, pleaded with the company to lay her off instead of me—to no avail. I've never been back. I do imagine the pall of cigarette smoke gone, the phone cords now tucked inside modular furniture, itself tucked into cubes, Dilbert style, and the building's inhabitants probably no longer punching time clocks, but they are still servants.

I was out of work for several months, finally finding employment on the East Coast. When not looking for work, I used the time to read deeply into organizational and management theory. My career eventually recovered from the Boeing layoff. I gained admittance to a Federal Aviation Administration (FAA) management intern program, and continued my research—happily now at government expense—attending every management course I could possibly wheedle my way into, including a course on "Management by Objectives" taught by a then obscure guy named Deming. Ed Deming, as many readers know, was the father of the quality movement. It was a few years later that he came to prominence as his ideas about quality control fed the Japanese technology explosion, dominating world markets.

Before the internet was established, I developed computer-based instruction for the FAA, networking 400 terminals around the country. Only the air traffic control system itself was bigger. I negotiated a consortium with the Army and Air Force to share mainframe computers and talked the Office of Air Traffic Control into piggybacking on their radar links so that my computer system had free cross-country phone service.

In 1984, I received the highly prized Secretary of Transportation Award for Excellence. I had proven to myself that I could play the bureaucracy. I had secured my position and could stick around, probably to climb the FAA management ladder, but somehow that prospect didn't excite me. I realized I was bored.

Fortuitously, for entirely other reasons, I was in the Netherlands to speak on computer-based training, met Gerard Endenburg, and discovered sociocracy. What followed was excitement mixed with many frustrations. I made many trips to Holland to learn about sociocracy in more depth. I followed Endenburg and other members of the Sociocratisch Centrum around the Dutch countryside and filled several notebooks. I left the FAA to work in computer project management for various government contractors so I had more flexibility to pursue my interest in sociocracy. I had a kind of parallel career while I deepened my understanding. I learned to read Dutch in order to gain access to the considerable literature not available in English.

The Idea of Equality

In my research I learned that except for a brief period in ancient Athens, and perhaps, in some preliterate societies, the notion that all people should be equal is relatively recent. Even the Athenian model allowed for slaves and excluded women.

The idea of full social equality first appears in the Peasants' Revolt in England in 1381. The decisive event came when Wat Tyler led about 200,000 peasants into London to demand better treatment for serfs and the right to participate in elections for members of Parliament.

Tyler was supported by John Ball, an itinerant priest who reasoned that we are all descended from Adam and Eve who were equal in the eyes of God and that the nobility was a later creation of the devil. A return to a more godly state, therefore, meant the need to get rid of the nobility. After burning many buildings, two prisons, capturing the Tower of London, and killing the archbishop of Canterbury, Tyler won many concessions from the teenaged King Richard II, including the abolition of rents and the elimination of serfdom and forced labor. But when Tyler was knifed to death in a scuffle with the Lord Mayor of London on a viewing stand in front of a crowd of thousands, the King granted a pardon to the peasants who had participated in the rebellion, everyone went home, and demands for equality disappeared.

During the English Civil War (1642 to 1649), the Levellers, led by English Puritan leader and Quaker, John Lilburne (~1614-1657), proposed a constitution for England that 150 years later became the basis for James Madison's Virginia Proposal and thus for the Constitution of the United States. It was unique in that it was not based on religious doctrine, proposed ending state support of the church, and advocated religious tolerance for all citizens. The Puritan military leader Oliver Cromwell (1599-1658), who overthrew and beheaded Charles I, squashed the Levellers and Lilburne died in prison. In 1660, Parliament once again recognized the monarchy.

About the same time, George Fox (1624-1691) started the Quaker religious movement which asserted that all people are of equal value in the eyes of God. Fox invented a bottom up form of organization based on achieving group unity before taking action. But the Quaker process remained a religious practice.

Democracy

Experimentation with egalitarian politics popped up again in the build-up to the American Revolution. This time it took root. The Declaration of Independence (1776) appeals strongly to the concept of natural law and self-determination. It is heavily influenced by the Act of Abjuration of the Dutch Republic, by the Discourses on Government of Algernon Sydney, to whose legacy Thomas Jefferson and John Adams were equally devoted, and by the English Bill of Rights. Some ideas and even some of the phrasing were taken directly from the writings of John Locke, particularly his second treatise on government, titled "Essay Concerning the true original, extent, and end of Civil Government."

The ripples of such extensive support for equal rights and individual freedom are still working themselves out—in the civil rights movement and the push for women's and gay rights. But the arena of society that has proven most resistant to this revolution of equality is employment. When one becomes employed, one loses rights that are recognized as self-evident in other spheres of life. By taking a job and accepting a check in exchange for labor, one becomes a servant with fewer rights than one had a few moments before. Neither businesses nor charitable organizations function according to egalitarian principles when one is on salary.

The sociocratic organization, the topic of this book, has the promise to change this condition and to bring to the world of employment the same egalitarian structures we enjoy in our personal lives.

Sociocracy

After I encountered Gerard Endenburg, I continued my traditional business career as a project manager, eventually leading as many as 180 people. We consistently received outstanding client ratings and achieved ISO 9000 quality certification. Even though I could not use all aspects of sociocracy in my work, I credit my understanding of sociocratic theory for these accomplishments. Meanwhile, I enrolled in a Master's program in quantitative sociology and wrote my thesis on the effects of sociocracy on Dutch workers. One of many things I found was that workers in Dutch sociocratic organizations have a statistically significantly higher level of commitment to their organization than their non-sociocratic counterparts.

Convinced that sociocracy did, in fact, yield the benefits claimed, I went through a rigorous process to become a certified sociocratic organizational adviser—the first native-English speaker to do so—and started a United States-based consulting business, finally abandoning my managerial career.

The sociocratic method, or more formally the sociocratic circle-organization method, is not a model for worker ownership or communal ownership; rather it reframes the whole concept of ownership and eliminates the master-servant relationship. In doing so, it better meets investors' needs for trust in strong management and for secure long-term investments. It better meets the needs of executives and managers for cooperation, loyalty, and trust by their staff. It better meets the needs of staff for respect and true inclusion, for enfranchisement in the organization. How it does that is the story of this book.

The following pages offer practical tools for bringing a truly egalitarian organization into being and for achieving the highest quality standards, and, oh yes, improving the traditional bottom line—productivity and profits.

CHAPTER TWO

Why We Need Another "-ocracy"
by Sharon Villines

I discovered sociocracy in 2002 at a regional workshop for cohousing communities, those hybrids of old-fashioned neighborhoods and condominiums that have been springing up across the United States since the 1980s. I had taken early retirement from university teaching in New York and moved into a community in Washington, DC, ostensibly to write. I was getting little done.

For two years I had been either working to organize the community or trying to understand why, despite being inclusive to a fault, our group, in my view, was so ineffective in meeting its own needs. Joining together from locations across the eastern Unites States, we had cooperatively designed and built our community, a combination of 43 townhouses and apartments with extensive common facilities including a kids' playroom, an exercise room, a laundry room, a dining room, a large professional kitchen, and a workshop. After move-in, however, we suddenly needed an organizational structure that could manage this multi-million dollar real estate complex and meet the needs of a community of families experiencing births, deaths, and major illnesses along with job losses and marriages. We had bylaws and an idea of how we wanted to function but the number of decisions that needed to be made was overwhelming, and of course, when it came right down to it, we were strangers. Less so than most new neighbors, but still strangers.

Typical of cohousing communities, we were using consensus as our method of decision-making. Consensus seeks approval from all members of the group to moving forward with a proposal. That meant that were constantly consulting everyone and holding many meetings in order to consult. The amount of time and energy that took was exhausting. With the seemingly constant need for decisions, I was increasingly frustrated that rather than waiting for the consensus process to unfold, more and more decisions were being either avoided altogether, made by default, or made by small teams or individuals by fiat. That I was one of the individuals making many of those decisions didn't make it any more acceptable to me. I wanted shared decisions.

Consensus

In the United States in the social upheavals of the late 1960's and early 1970s, many alternative organizations rejected majority vote because by definition a majority creates a minority. It emphasizes differences and forces participants to take sides rather than working together toward mutually beneficial solutions. Since women and people of color were minorities in most organizations, rule by majority vote excluded any chance of their being included equally. Consensus, on the other hand, seemed to put each individual on equal footing.

My first experience with consensus came in 1972 when I joined a group of parents to form a cooperative school for our children. We had many radical ideas about education—anti-sexist, anti-ageist, and anti-racist—essentially anti- anything that ignored the unique needs and abilities of the individual.

It was a new idea then for parents to just go off and start their own school, and we were having great difficulty finding space. We had no public funding or grants. We had no ability to guarantee even a year's worth of rent. One building finally offered us space on terms I don't remember. There were problems but we knew we could work them out—except for one woman who was sure this was a bad decision. We spent over four hours in a parent meeting, discussing well into the night. Many parents had to leave. Some could only stay because their children were asleep in a corner on a pile of coats. There were about 25 parents who wanted to rent the space and one who did not. That one woman represented our only parent of color and our only parent not holding a solid middle class job. We desperately wanted to keep her in the group and we equally desperately wanted to start the school in the space that we felt was our only option.

Failing to reach consensus, we agreed to meet again the next night. We left the room convinced that she would come around if she had more time. But she didn't. The next night, each of us walked back into the room understanding that she was right. Overnight, a sleepless night for many, we had come to realize that the demands the owner was making were unreasonable. Because this young welfare mom had stood her ground against a whole room of white professionals, we avoided what could easily have been a fatal mistake.

Reaching consensus on a hard decision created enormous power as well as satisfaction and harmony in the group. Once I had that experience it was difficult to settle for less. But that decision, and those that followed, took many, many hours of meetings. How many people had that level of commitment? And were able to sustain it? Not many.

Other cooperative ventures I joined or started during those years also did not. The food co-op, the Unitarian church committees, the lobbying groups, and feminist action groups worked on a sort of "soft consensus" in which they tried for agreement but moved on with the majority or the will of the leader if consensus could not be achieved quickly, usually in two meetings. The pattern was that consensus worked well in the early stages of an organization when there was high commitment to an ideal but less well as that commitment faded and the daily grind of operational decisions set in. Consensus alone provided no option to full-group decision-making. It gave us no guidance in delegating decisions or learning to be leaders or to trust leadership. It taught us nothing about delegating task or measuring results or analyzing needs.

By the time *Building United Judgment: A Handbook for Consensus Decision Making* (Avery 1981), the first guide to consensus decision-making, began to circulate in the early 1980s, I had moved away from groups that were even thinking about consensus.

Parliamentary Procedure

When I discovered cohousing, I found myself again sitting in meetings where long impassioned off-topic speeches were much in need of Points of Order and other equally impassioned but wrong-headed soliloquies needed Points of Information. But along with majority vote most groups using consensus had also rejected parliamentary procedure, namely Robert's *Rules of Order.*

Before I began working with consensus I had been lobbying with a progressive Unitarian group. I learned parliamentary procedure in 1971 when Bella Abzug, Gloria Steinem, and Betty Friedan held workshops during the founding of the National Women's Political Caucus. I remember a key session when Bella Abzug insisted that until women understood Robert's *Rules of Order* they could not progress in politics. You have to know the rules and when to use them.

During one session in an imposing legislative chamber, surrounded by mahogany paneling and gold leaf, the New York Radical Feminists were not able to adapt to the rules of debate. They started a ruckus on the floor by standing on benches and chanting. Frustration was growing on all sides until the able woman in charge said, "The Chair senses chaos on the floor and requests a five-minute recess to confer." She marched down to the center of the rebellion and when we resumed, the Radical Feminists presented their points of order in perfect form. Bella did everything but throw her hat in the air she was so happy. And Bella happy was a sight to behold.

Thirty years later, I was not able to find a parliamentarian who would work with me to design a system of governance that guaranteed inclusive decision-making along with an ordered process. And of course, parliamentary procedure alone could not build inclusiveness or equal access to governance. The "formal consensus process," advocated by C. T. Butler in *Conflict and Consensus* (1991) structures debate leading to consensus, but like parliamentary procedure, it essentially structures discussion of a proposal on the floor. It doesn't discuss how you function except as a committee of the whole.

One of the difficulties of consensus decision-making is that the only recognized structure is The Meeting. Committees, or the new "teams," can write proposals and make recommendations but the real meat of the organization only exists in a meeting of all members of the organization. The discussion is highly dependent on a good facilitator who is able to move the discussion forward. Historically, the Quaker Meeting with its "sense of the meeting" serves as the model for consensus decision-making but too often groups use consensus in an attempt to recreate that feeling of unity without making a commitment to anything resembling Quaker discipline. Groups also attempt to avoid any structure that might reintroduce either majority or minority rule; thus they oppose all hierarchy.

Now, actually living in a consensus community, I found that consensus decision-making was only the tip of the iceberg. The equally important questions were: How do you get to the decision? Who decides what needs a full group decision? Does everyone have to make all decisions? And how do you develop leadership when the only recognized leader is a facilitator who is expected to be neutral—to care nothing about the decision? These, I found, were even more perplexing issues than the actual process of reaching consensus. We had no leadership or structure that either built toward a decision or relieved us of the burden of making all decisions as a full group.

We had no governance structure to provide a context for decision-making. We had rules and regulations and teams and a board, but were they supporting or complimenting inclusive decisions? No, because they weren't making them easier—or inclusive.

And the group was growing. With the addition of many children and significant others, family-growing that had been postponed until the community was built and everyone moved in, we had grown to over 60 people (now in 2007, almost 80).

Governing Ourselves

In my community, and in hundreds of other intentional communities, utopian all, we are essentially rewriting the rules all the time. And it is painful. We are not, nor do we want to be, full time organizational development experts. We just want to live our lives, in a better way to be sure, but mostly, to just live.

After years of wallowing in these questions about consensus, effective organization, and world change—suffering the ill effects of both wallowing and not wallowing—I was ready to listen when John Buck said sociocracy is a way to govern ourselves that respects the equal value of people as individuals and that produces more equitable and effective organizations.

I wanted to know more and read everything I could find. There was very little written in English on sociocracy and what was available was written by a Dutch engineer. The translations were rough, and the language of physics and mathematics and systems thinking was foreign to me. As an artist, I had little background in physics or math.

What I knew of systems thinking had come from philosophy, not the technical sciences, but I found a depth of thinking and clarity of methodology that was better than anything else I had read. Further, *it was not just a theory*. It was a practical method of organization and decision making that was being used in professional associations as well as in boardrooms, in schools as well as in corporations, in intentional communities as well as breweries. It was giving a voice to nursing home attendants and beleaguered middle managers alike. It was producing more responsive, more productive, and happier organizations. *It was working.*

What I needed to know was how? That's when this book was born, out of a search to understand how and to explain it in plain English.

When I proposed a book to John, I knew he had expertise in sociocracy and management. I had the ability to explain concepts developed in twenty-five years of teaching and participating in cooperative and academic organizations, some of the most poorly structured organizations in existence. Together I felt we might be able to produce a book that would speak to a broad audience.

In the five years it took to complete this book, I found John to be unfailingly astute in responding to questions, applying sociocratic principles in new situations, and finding new ways to express ideas that at first fell on my artist's ears like dumb-bells. I learned a lot about governance, organizational theory, systems thinking, and much about the history of management and governance. This involved translating concepts from Dutch to English, from physics to every day language, and from scientifically accurate terminology with negative social connotations to words that expressed both the heart and science of a new governance method.

I hope this labor was well spent and that you will both enjoy and benefit from the ideas we have attempted to express clearly enough for you to improve your own organizations and to make them more inclusive, transparent, and accountable.

CHAPTER THREE

The History of Sociocratic Governance

The word *sociocracy* dates from the early nineteenth century with French philosopher and sociologist Auguste Comte and appears again late in the century with American sociologist Lester Frank Ward. It remained a theory, however, until the 1940s, when an internationally known Dutch peace activist and educator, Kees Boeke (pronounced *Case Boo-ka*), developed the first functional sociocratic system and used it to govern his residential school. In the 1970s, entrepreneur and electrical engineer Gerard Endenburg used cybernetics and systems thinking to develop Boeke's principles into a governance method that could be widely used. Today the Sociocratisch Centrum in Rotterdam supports continued development of sociocratic governance methods and trains consultants who implement them worldwide.

Auguste Comte

Auguste Comte (1798-1857) was born in the social and economic turmoil that followed the French Revolution. He is best known for his philosophy of positivism that rejects theology and metaphysics as the basis of knowledge. "Positive knowledge" is that based on natural, observable phenomena and verified empirically. Positivism became historically important because it provided the philosophical base for the emergence of scientific method in the nineteenth century.

In addition to the wars and political upheavals of this period, the Industrial Revolution had begun to fundamentally transform the European social structure, disrupting the stable agrarian culture that had been in place for centuries. With the monarchies gone or stripped of power and the control of the church beginning to crumble, society was adrift with people in all sectors disillusioned and lacking confidence. Believing solutions to social problems could be found using reasoning and analysis, Comte called for a science that would ensure a better future for all citizens. He called this new science *sociology* and further defined a social system in which all members of a society would participate in their own governance, *sociocracy*. Sociocracy would be built on both social ideals and scientific inquiry.

With the decreasing power of the church and the monarchy, Comte believed people had an opportunity for the first time to become self-sufficient and self-determining—to fully realize their essential human nature. For Comte human nature was characterized by reason, knowing, social cooperation, and altruistic feeling, but individuals were also products of their environment. Without an environment that supported these qualities, they would not succeed.

While Comte believed that social change would come from the workers, not owners, his own idea of a perfect society was heavily based on a hierarchy of authoritarian decision-making, not by kings or priests but by experts. He envisioned his sociocracy as an inclusive government, but reflecting the contemporary social structures, he was unable to envision it without a ruling hierarchy. His society was to be centrally governed by social scientists. (Comte 1853)

Comte is often criticized for being overly systematic and dogmatic and today would be criticized for his concepts of social control, but as a theorist and scientist, Comte changed the basis on which knowledge was measured by seeking scientific facts that enabled the discovery of the laws of nature. His ideas strongly influenced English thinkers like David Hume who in turn influenced the course of American political and economic thought and the new democracy then emerging in the United States.

Lester Frank Ward

Frank Ward (1843-1913), the father of sociology in America, continued the thinking of Comte in conceiving of an ideal society as a sociocracy ordered by scientific thought rather than by divine right, inheritance, or political power. Where Comte placed a scientific priesthood in control of society, Ward envisioned an academy of social scientists that would advise the government. Where Comte prescribed an ideal social structure as the controlling force, Ward believed that the successful individual, supported and enabled by the social structure, was responsible for human progress. He extolled the rugged individual who pulled himself up by the bootstraps and took advantage of what society offered. As a clerk who obtained college degrees in botany and law by studying evenings, Ward himself was such a person.

After obtaining his degrees, Ward worked as a paleontologist and archeologist for the federal government. He also became a prominent sociologist and at the age of 65 accepted a professorship at Brown University. He was elected the first president of the International Institute of Sociology in 1903 and first president of the American Sociological Society in 1906.

Ward believed the uniquely human characteristics of mind and purpose evolved out of our physical nature, but once consciousness and intelligence emerged, mind and purpose were responsible for social progress. Nature left to its own devices was inefficient and grandly wasteful in its use of resources. A codfish, he said, must produce 1,000,000 young fish so that two may survive. The human mind, on the other hand, is purposeful and superior, and through knowledge, capable of controlling nature. Therefore, the proper focus of sociology was not the study of social structures, as Comte advocated, but the study of remarkable individuals.

> My thesis is that the subject matter of sociology is human achievement. It is not what men are, but what they do. It is not the structure, but the function. Sociologists are nearly all working in the department of social anatomy, when they should turn their attention to social physiology. (Ward 1902)

Rather than viewing the materialistic environment as a limiting and controlling factor as Marx did, Ward saw it as something to be improved. The mind and consciousness made human society capable of bringing material culture under its control. While he condemned the tyranny of the individual, Ward believed that the power of society was to be found in the individual. The individual "should be praised, and even imitated." If society could be guided by the will and the intellect of all individuals combined, society would become the greatest force ever known. He believed that the individual had a lesson to teach politicians as well. In the gaming environment of politics, politicians forget the real interests of society and

> ... lose their grasp on real issues, forget even their own best interest, which, however selfish, would be a far safer guide, and the general result usually is that these are neglected and nations continue in the hands of mere politicians who are easily managed by the shrewd representatives of wealth. [Under sociocracy,] society would inquire in a business way without fear, favor, or bias, into everything that concerned its welfare, and if it found opportunities, it would improve them. In a word, society would do under the same circumstances just what an intelligent individual would do. It would further, in all possible ways, its own interests." (Ward 1902)

Ward wrote extensively about education as the primary force in the progress of society and believed that the unequal distribution of knowledge was responsible for many (if not all) social problems. It is in education that we see the next developments in sociocracy.

Kees Boeke: Democracy as It Might Be

What moved sociocracy from the ideals of Comte and Ward to a practical application was dissatisfaction with the flawed democracies that prevailed in Europe in the early twentieth century (the same flaws that Ward decried in American democracy) and the crisis caused by World War II. Like Ward, Kees Boeke (1884-1966), a Dutch civil engineer, Quaker, and pacifist, saw education as a primary tool in establishing peace. In 1914, Boeke was in Lebanon and Syria establishing workshops where children of all cultures and religions could study together to understand each other's cultures. When war broke out, Boeke was forced to go back to The Netherlands where he joined the Bilthoven Movement, an effort to build a new social order, and founded an international brotherhood to work for peace called Paco, Esperanto for *peace.*

In 1926, Boeke founded a private residential school, the Werkplaats Kindergemeenschap, the Children's Community Workshop. There he developed a sociocratic environment to implement the values he felt would lead to a peaceful society and allow human beings to develop naturally.

As early as 1933, Jewish teenagers were being sent out of Germany to Britain and the Netherlands for safety. When informed that they had no school, Boeke set up a special classroom. One of the teachers hired to teach them was Joop Westerweel. In 1942, Westerweel organized an underground and smuggled 200 Jews into Belgium, then to France, then Switzerland or Spain. In 1944, Westerweel was captured, imprisoned, and tortured, and when he refused to name his contacts, was executed. Boeke was also arrested but without corroborating evidence was ultimately released.

When the Germans arrested Boeke, he carried in his pocket a manuscript, *No Dictatorship*. In May 1945, the month the Canadians liberated The Netherlands, that manuscript was published as *Sociocracy: Democracy As It Might Be* (see Appendix B). In it Boeke presents the deficiencies of democracy as he saw it implemented:

> We are so accustomed to majority rule as a necessary part of democracy that it is difficult to imagine any democratic system working without it. It is true that it is better to count heads than to break them, and democracy, even as it is today, has much to recommend it as compared with former practices. But the party system has proved very far from providing the ideal democracy of people's dreams. Its weaknesses have become clear enough: endless debates in Parliament, mass meetings in which the most primitive passions are aroused, the overruling by the majority of all independent views, capricious and unreliable election results, government action rendered inefficient by the minority's persistent opposition. Strange abuses also creep in. Not only can a party obtain votes by deplorably underhand methods, but also, as we all know, a dictator can win an election with an "astonishing" majority by intimidation. (Boeke 1945)

Boeke's interest in sociocracy, what he thought democracy should be, came from inquiry into the nature of people working together in ways that preserved the equality and integrity of each person. He envisioned a sociocratic society as "a real community-democracy, an organization of the community by the community itself." In his school, he created a self-governing community of almost four hundred students and teachers.

Boeke had been active in the International Center for Progressive Schools (ICPS) and his own school became internationally known in the progressive schools movement and was attended by three of the Dutch royal children. Queen Juliana, who reigned in The Netherlands from 1948 to 1980, believed that the royal children should live and be educated with other children. She and her children had spent World War II in Canada but on their return, with all the best schools in Europe to choose from, she chose Boeke's.

Boeke is perhaps best known outside of The Netherlands for his book, *Cosmic View: The Universe in 40 Jumps* (1957), which served as the basis for the film by Charles and Ray Eames *The Power of Ten* (1968) which is now the basis of an extensive interactive web site at www.powersof10.com and inspired the IMAX film the *Cosmic Voyage* (1996). The book presents a series of forty pictures composed to help children develop a sense of scale and to understand themselves in relation to the universe. Each picture jumps, in exact scale, in powers of 10, from a picture of a girl outdoors in a chair up to a view of her neighborhood, then to her country, and so on until the pictures reach the edge of the universe. Then they move back from the girl in the chair into microscopic views of her skin tissues and finally, under a magnification of ten million, the nucleus of a sodium atom. In the forward, Boeke said:

> At school we are introduced to many different spheres of existence, but they are often not connected with each other, so that we are in danger of collecting a large number of images without realizing that they all join together in one great whole. It is therefore important in our education to find the means of developing a wider and more connected view of our world and a truly cosmic view of the universe and our place in it. (Boeke 1957)

The First Application of Sociocracy

Boeke began by adapting the Society of Friends system of self-governance that rejected majority voting in favor of full inclusiveness. He believed his system could be applied on a national and international scale once everyone understood that the problem with social organization was a matter of discipline and respect for the group. If groups were expected to learn self-discipline the way an individual had to learn self-discipline, there would be no need for an executive committee or ruling class.

There are three fundamental rules underlying the system. The first is that the interests of all members must be considered, the individual bowing to the interests of the whole. Secondly, solutions must be sought which everyone can accept: otherwise, no action can be taken. Thirdly, all members must be ready to act according to these decisions when unanimously made. (Boeke 1945)

Boeke felt these rules were nothing more than concern for one's neighbor, "where love is, there will be a spirit in which real harmony is possible." In the political party system, disagreements are accentuated because the parties desire to accentuate their unique differences and to sharpen their divisions. In a sociocratic system, where "*agreement* must be reached, it activates a common search that brings the whole group nearer together." Rather than the expected stalemates and lack of progress that one might expect in this situation, Boeke found the mutual trust and desire to act in the best interests of the group "leads inevitably to progress."

In Boeke's plan, larger governance systems would be composed of representatives from neighborhood groups who would also be chosen by agreement, someone in whom everyone had confidence. Boeke found that in practice "when representation is not a question of power but of trust, the choice of a suitable person can be made fairly easily and without unpleasantness." (Boeke 1945) The third principle, that all members must agree to act when agreement is reached, means the decision is binding on all who have participated in making it. If a group's representatives have agreed, the group is bound by that agreement. Boeke recognized that the size of self-governing groups was important:

> It must be big enough for personal matters to give way to an objective approach to the subject under discussion, but small enough not to be unwieldy, so that the quiet atmosphere needed can be secured. For meetings concerned with general aims and methods a group of about forty has been found the most suitable. But when detailed decisions have to be made, a small committee will be needed of three to six persons or so. (Boeke 1945)

Boeke pointed out that there were many, many groups functioning this way—by soliciting common agreement rather than voting and that if such a group voted, it would be an indication that the group was not functioning well. This process was formalized in his school.

Boeke had personally participated in many Quaker Meetings of over a thousand people who had functioned by reaching agreement together. Sociocracy, like the tradition of Quaker Meetings, needed to be learned, but Boeke believed that the Quaker experience proved that it could be done: "We shall be able to learn this art and acquire a tradition that will make possible the handling of more difficult questions." In his school, the process began in "talkovers" or weekly meetings that included both teachers and students, acting equally. Boeke envisioned that all of society could be structured the same way. Kees taught the children in his school to be responsible for helping guide their own education and they flourished. One of his students was Gerard Endenburg.

Gerard Endenburg

Gerard Endenburg (1933-) was the first person to define a set of principles that allowed sociocracy to be applied apart from religious or closely-knit heterogeneous communities. Rather than a social theorist like Comte, Ward, and Boeke, Endenburg was an inventor, engineer, and entrepreneur. His interest was in practical application, in making things work and, particularly, in making them work better. Since his education was in the physical sciences rather than the social sciences, Endenburg was able to analyze organizational structures and social interactions from completely different perspectives—physics and mathematics.

Endenburg was the son of political activists Anna and Gerardus Endenburg. Anna Endenburg was a well-known actor who also went about the country giving fiery speeches advocating radical reform. After World War II to the dismay of their socialist friends, the Endenburgs decided that the only way to prove that their egalitarian principles were sound was to demonstrate that they were economically viable. To do this, they established Endenburg Electrotechniek.

The Endenburgs' decision to set up a company was both insightful and fundamentally important. At a time when socialist parties were winning control of national governments throughout Europe, the Endenburgs were not celebrating. They could see that the ideas they had struggled for were inadequate and trapped in "either-or" thinking. The Endenburgs wanted a more inclusive, "both-and" society that would simultaneously understand the needs of both labor and management, and both the governed and the government.

The Endenburgs were aware of contemporary management theories as well as political theories and anticipated many concepts of participative management that developed later. They formed Endenburg Electrotechniek to be both a successful business and to demonstrate management concepts. Originally organized to sell lamps and electrical parts, the company now does heavy electrical installations on oil rigs, ships, nuclear reactors, and large buildings. The company recently celebrated its fiftieth anniversary and remains a thriving enterprise, an incubator for new ideas, and the first sociocratically organized corporation.

Cybernetics and Thinking by Analogy

Gerard Endenburg finished his high school studies under Kees Boeke and went to a technical college where the instructor was an autocrat ruling the classroom. The students were quiet or even sullen and did not form cooperative groups. Some students were even bullies. Endenburg was amazed but adapted quickly. Boeke had taught him that behavior is molded by the prevailing social structure.

Endenburg was attracted to engineering, attempting once as a teenager to invent a personal helicopter. The resulting machine managed to rise a few feet off the ground, and the roar of the engine disturbed the neighbors for blocks around. In college, he focused on electrical engineering and then spent his compulsory military service on assignment in Germany where he instructed radar technicians, teaching among other things, cybernetics, the new science of communication and control that had been developed during WW II in work with anti-aircraft missiles.

After military service, Endenburg worked for Philips Electronics, and quickly displayed his technical genius by inventing the flat speaker that is still used today in personal radios and other hand-held electronics such as cell phones. The invention reinforced what he had learned from cybernetics: there is tremendous power in thinking by analogy. He developed the speaker first by thinking about his experience with vibration in purely mechanical systems. He analyzed the general cybernetic principles involved and then applied them to the electronic speaker problem. Later he worked in the reverse direction, solving mechanical problems with heavy valves in ships by making analogies to electronic systems where the parallel problem had been solved.

Endenburg's father interrupted Gerard's career at Philips, challenging him to test his management skills. His father had bought a small, failing electronics company and suggested that Endenburg try to turn it from loss to profit. Endenburg succeeded in less than a year, and the company was merged with Endenburg Electrotechniek. Encouraged by Kees Boeke and challenged by friends to apply his understanding of cybernetics to management, Endenburg eventually took over as general manager of Endenburg Electrotechniek. The charge from his parents was that the company continue to be a living laboratory for new ideas in business management.

From 1968 to 1970, Endenburg focused on understanding management. Management is essentially the art of organizing people analogous to the way an engineer organizes power and materials. The objective in each case is to create the strongest, most powerful system possible. He observed that technical science and management science used many similar terms, words that he could define precisely in the technical context but couldn't define so clearly in management of people: power, tension, tolerance, variance, limits, correction, measurement, resistance, capacity, stress, dynamics, systems, etc.

"No one can precisely define these terms in a human system. So, how can anyone manage effectively?" Was there the possibility here for thinking by analogy? "I know how to steer power in mechanical and electrical systems," he reasoned. "How can I steer power in human systems?" (Buck 2003)

The cybernetic theory that Endenburg had applied during his military service was fundamental to Endenburg's work, specifically the work of American mathematician Norbert Wiener (1894-1964) who specialized in electronics engineering and was a pioneer in communication and control in electronic systems. Weiner had coined the term "cybernetics" in his book *Cybernetics, or Control and Communication in the Animal and the Machine* (1948), widely recognized as one of the most important books of contemporary scientific thinking. It was cybernetics that first taught Endenburg to think by analogy so that he could study and transfer knowledge from mechanical to electrical systems. Now he used it to design a system that would work in human systems. Endenburg's ability to apply analogical thinking in the social and management sciences was an essential key in his ability to develop a model for a universally practical application of sociocratic theory.

Systems Thinking

Endenburg's design of sociocratic organizations also reflects the work of systems thinking including Kenneth Boulding, John Forbes Nash, and Ilya Prigogine. British American economist Kenneth Boulding (1910-1993) studied the ethical implications of large scale organizations and human economic behavior as part of the larger interconnected social system. As Comte and Boeke had also stressed, Boulding found that to understand behavior, we must understand the general system in which it exists. If we want to change behavior, we need to change the system. Systems thinking was thus the first theoretical model to recognize human behavior as part of an open system, meaning that it is affected by the environment in which it exists.

In an open system of interconnected parts, small events can cause large changes and a change in one area can adversely affect another area. A system is a dynamic and complex whole that interacts as a structured functional unit. It may be composed of parts seeking equilibrium but can also exhibit chaotic or exponential growth or decay. Ilya Prigogine (1917-2003) won the Nobel Prize in Chemistry in 1977 for his work in dissipative structures and his work stimulated research in self-organizing systems that move from seemly chaotic to orderly conditions behavior. John Forbes Nash's work in game theory influenced Endenburg's design of compensation systems, which we will discuss later.

The Investor-Manager-Worker Cooperative

The first challenge Endenburg tackled at Endenburg Electrotechniek was creating a financial compensation structure for the company's workers, managers, and investors that would encourage everyone to be an entrepreneur, to trust their individual sense of rightness and take responsibility for the success of the corporation. He expected such a system to increase both creativity and profitability. Following the principle of "both-and" thinking, he developed a system of fixed and variable compensation. Unlike stock options, these incentives were cash payments directly linked to performance. Fixed compensation reflected the fair market value of each person's training and expertise or the amount of each stockholder's investment. Variable compensation was tied to productivity. The short- and long-term variable compensation reflected each worker, manager, or investor's contribution to company profits or losses.

Cooperatives and employee-owned companies are difficult to capitalize and manage, and to avoid their problems, Endenburg wanted an investor-manager-worker cooperative. He viewed profit as a summary measurement of how well a company is doing, not as a goal in itself. Everyone, as an entrepreneur, needed to be able to feel both positive and negative effects of this measurement in order to be responsible for their part in producing it. This system, which we will discuss in detail later, has remained in place at Endenburg Electrotechniek to this day.

Decision Making by Consent

For workers to be true entrepreneurs, there had to be a practical way for them to have a meaningful voice in determining both short-term and long-term strategies. How could workers, management, and investors make decisions together as partners without paralyzing the decision-making process? Consensus, as Boeke used it in his school, and sense of the meeting, which the Quakers used, were based on many years of learning and thinking together, and on shared values. In a corporation, many decisions require fast responses from widely diverse groups of people. Neither Boeke's consensus nor sense of the meeting agreements would work in a corporation.

On a three-week personal retreat Endenburg wrestled with this problem, going over everything he knew about cybernetic principles and what they had to say about making decisions. The familiar forms of decision-making—autocratic, majority vote, and supra-majority vote—were just points on a continuum. None were satisfactory for an investor-manager-worker cooperative because none of them protected the interests of all the parties, and all were vulnerable to manipulation. Most important, none of them ensured that each person's interests would be protected equally, especially during crises.

He struggled for the entire three weeks of his retreat and finally gave up, concluding that there was no answer. He packed his bags and started loading up his car, and then the answer hit him: *consent!*

In the technical sciences, all elements of an operational system work together by consent, the absence of paramount objections. If one part of a system is stressed to the point of breaking down, a paramount objection, the system does not work. All parts must be able to function for the entire system to function. Endenburg had defined his first governing principle: consent governs decision-making, in particular, policy decisions.

Boeke's basic concepts, those Endenburg was trying to implement in a new context, were based on the principle that if we first loved and respected each other, problems could be resolved peacefully. The principle of consent respected Boeke's intentions and allowed people to make decisions together *without* the prerequisite of love and trust.

Krings, Rings, Circles, or Roundtables?

Where would decision-making by consent take place? Most organizations, certainly corporations, reflect the hierarchical structure of work. All work can be placed on a continuum from concrete, tangible actions to more abstract decisions. In an authoritarian structure, managers and supervisors make the more abstract policy decisions and direct production or the delivery of services. Gardening, for example, requires both concrete work, the digging of dirt and pulling of weeds, and abstract work, the planning, deciding what plants will be placed where. How could workers meet to make policy decisions if day-to-day, operational decisions were, of necessity, controlled by a manager or supervisor?

Endenburg's solution was to create a new governance structure that extends the governing powers usually accorded to a board of directors to all levels of the organization. This structure is composed of groups, called circles, in which managers, supervisors, and workers meet as peers to make policy decisions by consent. Each circle has its own aim and plans its own work to ensure productivity and profitability.

The word *circle* is a compromise translation of the Dutch *kring*, which literally translates as *ring* or *circle* but also includes the meaning of *arena*. A kring is an arena in which events happen, or in this case, where decisions are made. The English translation is difficult since we do not have an analogous word. *Circle* is a close translation but its connotations do not suggest serious decisions. We might use the word *ring* except for the negative connotations of criminal activity as in "ring of smugglers" and "ring leader."

The word *roundtable* is familiar in English-speaking organizations and carries with it the tradition of serious discussion among equals. King Arthur assembled roundtable meetings so his knights could discuss and resolve issues without fighting over status. Today government and industry convene roundtables, or "think tanks," to address policy concerns. We have such organizations as the Philanthropy Roundtable, The Berkeley Roundtable on the International Economy, the Sustainable Community Roundtable, The Roundtable on Religion and Social Welfare. *Roundtable*, however, no longer has associations with binding decisions. So, we use the word *circle* because it is more specific. Keep the image of the roundtable as a discussion between peers when you read *circle*.

Double-Linking

The number of people who can attend a circle meeting is obviously limited. How could large numbers of people make consent decisions? How could circles make decisions that affected more than one circle? To solve this problem Endenburg developed the concept of double-linking.

Rensis Lickert, in his two seminal works *New Patterns of Management* (1961) and *The Human Organization* (1967), introduced the idea of the manager as a link between levels of the organization. The manager exercises this linking responsibility by communicating from the top of the organization to the bottom and from the bottom to the top. Using cybernetic principles, Endenburg concluded that one person, a single link between levels of the organization, could not carry information in two directions at once. He conceived of a second link, this one carrying information from the bottom to the top. Each circle would have a leader, Lickert's downward link, and a second link, a person elected to be responsible for carrying information upward. With this network of double-links, hundreds of circles could be linked into a network that efficiently carries information up and down the organization.

This idea of double-linking is unique to the sociocratic method, and as we will see later, is integral to quality control because it creates feedback loops that are necessary to create and maintain self-correcting organizations.

Electing People to Functions and Tasks

From the beginning, Endenburg intended that circles would use consent to elect people to functions and tasks. Since the choice of a person to do a job is one of the most important decisions a circle could make, it would be made by consent. In practice, he found that concept needed to be emphasized separately because people were reluctant to do it, so he created the fourth governance principle to support them. This process has proven to be a powerful way to bond members of a circle.

Testing the Method

During the first half of the 1970s, Endenburg proceeded to test these four foundational concepts—policy decisions made by consent, circles for the making and execution of policy decisions, double-linking between circles, and the election of people to functions and tasks by consent—and Endenburg Electrotechniek prospered. This attracted newspaper attention and Endenburg began to explain his sociocracy to a few other organizations. Then in 1976 came a shock. The Dutch shipping industry shut down, collapsing under the pressure of competition from Japanese ship builders. Nearly half of Endenburg Electrotechniek's workforce was employed in the shipyards doing the heavy wiring for the ships' electrical systems.

Endenburg called an emergency meeting of the Top Circle (including the board of directors) to plan for a layoff. Layoffs in Holland are more complex than in the United States because the government must concur. Two of the four outside directors told Endenburg that he needed to set his sociocratic experiment aside because now he had important business to deal with. Drastic layoffs were announced for the shipping department.

As the news spread, a machinist who worked in the specialized electrical-cabinet fabrication shop called an emergency meeting of the Fabrication Circle, which was not targeted in the planned layoff. "We don't have to lay off the guys in Ships," he said. "The company has built up a strategic reserve for emergencies, and this is an emergency. I propose we put coats and ties on those shipyard workers, give them some training in marketing, and send them out to get more business." The Fabrication Circle supported his idea and, using the flexibility of the double-linking principle, selected him as a special representative to the company's General Circle to present this idea.

The General Circle, which included representatives from the company's other production and administrative circles, made a few modifications in the proposal and then selected him as a representative to the Top Circle. He duly made his proposal to the second Top Circle meeting called to address layoffs. A heavy discussion ensued and the two skeptical outside directors resigned, saying that the machinist had no business being there.

Finally, the Top Circle adopted the machinist's proposal with modifications. The shipyard workers were trained to go out and make marketing calls, and within a few weeks had brought in enough new orders to permit most of the layoffs to be canceled. The company emerged from the crisis stronger because it retained its skilled workers, strengthened company morale, *and* became more diversified.

Endenburg now had proof that the sociocratic method worked. It could be unusually flexible and produce highly effective and creative thinking. He had developed a governance system that encouraged leadership to emerge anywhere in the organization and to be recognized. It allowed a complex organization to function according to the same principles of self-interest and willpower that an individual uses to achieve success—and it ensured protection of the interests of all workers, owners, and investors.

The Free Organization

Endenburg then turned to the fundamental question of power in organizations. Consent was, in fact, not the fundamental basis of decision making in his company. As majority stockholder he could decide, at any time, to sell it, close it, or revert to autocratic management. He still held the ultimate power. After numerous discussions with his lawyers and accountants, the organization became its own owner. As majority stockholder Endenburg had stockholder rights and as CEO he had the rights of the CEO but he no longer had "life or death" control over the organization—or its employees.

Legally, a corporation has the rights of a person because it exists as a legal entity, but it is also owned and is thus a slave to its owner. To the extent that its employees are dependent on the corporation, they are also slaves. Endenburg Electrotechniek and its workers are no longer enslaved. The company is also protected from hostile takeovers and cannot, along with its employees, be bought or sold. It can consent to merge with other organizations, or to disband, but only if the organization itself, with the consent of its participants, decides to sell, close, or change.

Endenburg has now retired from the management of Endenburg Electrotechniek and devotes his time to consulting and teaching sociocracy at the University of Maastricht where he is a professor in the school of business. He founded the Sociocratisch Centrum in Rotterdam to continue developing methods for applying sociocratic principles. The Centrum consults with organizations internationally to help them organize sociocratically.

Endenburg Electrotechniek recently moved to a larger building and continues to be a premier example of a successful sociocratic corporation. Since Endenburg published his first pamphlet, *Sociocracy: A Reasonable Ideal*, in 1974, the organizing principles and the company have been the subject of many studies including doctoral theses, quality certifications, and government reviews. The Netherlands government has amended its labor regulations to exempt sociocratic organizations from the requirement to have works councils, which are similar to in-house labor unions, because sociocracy protects workers' interests much better than the councils.

PART II

The Science of Sociocratic Governance

INTRODUCTION

Rewiring Organizational Power

☙❦❧

To understand how sociocratic organizations govern themselves so effectively, let's look more closely at what an organization is, or is intended to be. The word *organization* derives from the Latin *organum* meaning "tool or instrument," and the Greek *organon*. For example, the heart, an organ, is a tool that the body uses to circulate blood and oxygen. The suffix *-ize* means "to cause to be or to become," and the suffix *–ation*, "an action or the result of an action." Thus *to organize* is "to cause to become a tool." A human organization is the result of people coming together to become a tool to accomplish a task, a task that one person could not accomplish alone.

In our complex lives, very little can be accomplished alone. Even subsistence farming requires a goodly number of people to plow, plant, harvest, cook, weave, and barter. Building cars or producing films, just two examples, are even more complex and their technologies intricate and interdependent. National and international markets mean simple goods like milk and vegetables now have long supply lines that may require a farmer to understand the regulations of many governments—local, national, and international.

In modern societies, our ability to work together has created powerful organizations. While there is still hunger and illness, on the whole we live much longer, with less disease and discomfort and with many more luxuries, than at any time in history. We educate, specialize, and coordinate at a level of expertise and complexity that previous generations would have found incomprehensible. Our banks, utilities,

51

schools, manufacturers, and hospitals are vast webs of coordination that make all this possible.

Without good governance, however, flawed and predatory policies, illustrated by recent headlines about collapse at Enron, failures at the FBI, abuse and neglect at Walter Reed Army Hospital, and the wholesale exporting of jobs to countries that allow child labor work against our best efforts. The same organizations that bring us security, freedom, and wealth can also bring us poverty, alienation, and economic collapse. Sometimes the goals of our organizations conflict with, even replace, our own. As Prince Charles, the future King of England, said, "I was about ten when I realized I was trapped."

Just as royal families have not abdicated their privileges, however, neither are we suggesting that we abandon our comfortable lifestyles. What we are suggesting is that we need to become citizens in our own organizations. We need governance structures that enable us to participate as full partners to correct and control them because organizational failures are most often failures in governance—in policy making, enforcement, or oversight.

What Does It Mean to Govern?

The questions governance addresses are: What is the aim of the organization? How will this aim be achieved? Who makes decisions? How are priorities set? Or considered? How is money spent?

The meanings of *to govern* include "to rule," "to regulate," "to sway or influence," "to direct or guide," and "to hold in check, curb, bridle." All these meanings derive from the original meaning in several Latin-based languages: "to steer" from the Middle English, *governe*; French, *governer*; Portuguese, *governar*; Spanish, *gobernar*; Italian, *governare*; Latin, *gobernre*. All these variations originally meant "to steer a vessel." Thus sociocratic governance is a method of steering an organization toward its aim, of adjusting from moment to moment in response to changing conditions. The importance of governance, of steering, is greater today than ever before because we need new methods and new understandings in order to guide our increasingly complex organizations.

Rewiring Our Organizations

Sociocratic principles, based on the scientifically derived methods of cybernetics, systems thinking, and complexity theory, value each human being and the importance of the individual as an essential participant in an organization. Various political theories, like socialism and communism, have attempted to correct "the excesses of capitalism" by removed private ownership and transferring production to the state. Sociocratic governance works within a capitalist market and supports a free economy. While its methods produce revolutionary results, they do not require a revolution. They can be introduced gradually and do not interfere with functions or production although they greatly enhance it. They support good leadership and stable functioning.

Sociocratic governance does not throw the baby out with the bath water by rejecting what has gone before. It incorporates the traditional concerns of managing successful organizations—good decision-making, leadership, tactical and strategic planning, quality control, and financial stability.

In Part II we present the principles and methods sociocracy uses to structure and govern our organizations and examine the underlying science on which they are based. The questions we will be asking in relation to organizations are: What is *decision making*? What does it mean to *decide*? What is *leading*? What is *doing*? What is *measuring and correcting*? While these may seem like philosophical questions, and they are, they are also very practical ones.

CHAPTER FOUR

Inclusive Decision-Making

If you were starting an organization, one of your first tasks would be to decide who could make decisions; this would determine how your organization would be governed. Should it be a monarchy ruled by your family and their descendents? A democracy ruled by majority vote? If so, who will be allowed to vote?

Or would it be an autocracy with you as the autocrat? Perhaps as a benevolent autocrat who uses a participatory management style?

If it were a sociocracy, everyone directly affected by a decision would be involved in making that decision. Thus, instead of the board of directors or the owner constituting the governing body, it would include all the members of the organization. For many of us this feels impossible. How can an organization maintain daily functioning and allow everyone to be making decisions? The answer lies in a new and elegant governance structure.

Strong organizations are characterized by deep commitment. If every member is aligned with the aim of the organization and works whole-heartedly toward it, the organization is more likely to be effective, productive, and extremely powerful. If one person, or one department, falters, the whole organization will be less effective. To prevent such faltering, sociocratic organizations require that policy decisions be made with the participation and consent of those they most affect.

While this may seem unworkable, consent is actually one of our most common decision-making methods. Groups form, function, and dissolve by consent all the time. Many have short-term goals and are small, heterogeneous groups that arrange a holiday celebration for a few friends, play poker on Tuesday nights, or set up a schedule of play dates for children. These are decisions between friends who have probably made many decisions together. For many of us, these are our most pleasant experiences with decision-making. We have a clear aim and we are working with people we trust.

But in large organizations where people do not know each other, do not work closely together, and may have a variety of aims, we normally resort to autocratic decision-making. People, usually managers, make the day-to-day operational decisions and the most important policy decisions are reserved for a board of directors. Maintaining and building commitment in such an organization is very difficult. One reason is that often, none of the people who make the decisions have operational responsibilities and may be several organizational levels removed from those who implement their decisions.

Sociocratic organizations structure decision-making very differently. To ensure both the quality of decisions and the commitment to execute them, decisions are made by those who must implement them. This ensures more than participation; it ensures enfranchisement, freedom to object. To understand how unique this structure is we need to look at the history of governance and decision-making.

Authoritarian Decision-Making

The first complex human organizations were theocratic autocracies in which leaders made decisions based on their interpretation of the desires of gods. A vestige of these theocratic roots can be seen when power is asserted in the use of ceremony and formal dress; robes for judges, intricate titles for nobility and military officers, special music to accompany entrances, and other reminders of religious rituals.

Although some kings were considered divine into the twentieth century, social revolutions began to overthrow monarchies in the eighteenth century, demanding citizens' rights. Ironically, because non-royal citizens then gained the right to own property, authoritarian structures continued to flourish in the workplace. After the Industrial Revolution, citizens could vote but were still working fourteen-hour days. Factories employed children as young as six who worked alongside adults, often fed at their machines with no breaks. Authority to require these conditions was grounded not in divine right, but in property rights. Ownership became the new king.

As early as 1815 when Robert Owen, a British factory owner, wrote *Observations on the Effect of the Manufacturing System*, reformers were advocating worker cooperatives. Owen's own system included worker control but like similar proposals, it lacked a governance structure that protected the interests of both owners and workers and was thus unworkable. Although the new labor movement adopted his ideas for building worker-friendly environments, there was no change in autocratic governance or in the rights of owners.

With new, more democratic governments, political freedom was still economically empty.

Efficient Decision-Making

As corporations grew in size and number and developed inter-dependent relationships, leaders in government and business began to search for more stability, less friction, and more profit. In 1835, Charles Babbage, a pioneer in modern computing and management theory, advocated the efficiency of decisions based on objective data. The decision maker was to collect data and the workers were elements in the mechanical systems to be measured.

This approach grew more sophisticated with American mechanical engineer Frederick Winslow Taylor, a professor at Dartmouth, developed the time and motion study, and in 1911 popularized the term "scientific management." Often disparaged as "Taylorism," his method became famous when he measured the movements required to lay bricks or shovel coal in order to reduce wasteful human variation. For example, he designed shovels that varied in size and shape to carry the most efficient load of 21 pounds of different kinds of materials. Frank and Lillian Gilbreth popularized Taylorism first in the best-selling novel and then in the film *Cheaper by the Dozen* (1950) in which a family is organized on the principles of efficiency that included precise descriptions of exact tasks, often to be repeated endlessly by a child.

Taylor believed that a cooperative relationship between management and workers was necessary, but his methods were as autocratic as they were specific. The role of the manager was to decide and that of the worker to follow orders. The result of this attitude was that a manager who asked for workers' thoughts about their work or allowed individual human variations risked being considered weak or inviting insubordination.

Henry Ford standardized both his product and his production line in such an extreme manner that it was called "Fordism." First, he designed and produced a car in great quantities, in identical models, in one color—black, and then he invented "minute management" by measuring and analyzing each minute of a worker's time. Using those measurements, he simplified and fragmented tasks, de-skilling them to reduce the time required to do each step. Each worker then needed to learn only one small skill and was required to do the same action all day long. To make this possible Ford invented the moving assembly line. This reduced the time required to produce the chassis of his car from twelve hours and twenty-eight minutes to ninety-three "man minutes." (Zuboff 2002, 45)

Charlie Chaplin's film *Modern Times* (1936) satirizes Fordism. Inspired by a tour of the Ford plant in River Rouge, Chaplin portrays a frantic factory worker on an assembly line trying to keep up with a conveyer belt moving at an ever-faster pace. He ends up in a mental hospital. Ford's workers did essentially the same—they left in droves. In 1913, the year of the first moving assembly line, turnover was 380%. By the end of the year, Ford had to hire 963 workers to keep 100. He had to pay workers so much to keep them and cut his prices so deeply that his profit on each car was only $2.00. (Zuboff 2002)

Ford used the same principles to reduce management roles and ultimately lost his market when consumers began demanding more variety in car design. Because he had effectively eliminated all initiative and creativity, he had no managers or designers who could develop new models or manage new plants. Ford had structured decision-making so autocratically that he could not decentralize and diversify to meet consumer demand.

Consultative Decision-Making

In the management sciences in the 1920s, Mary Parker Follett was alone in suggesting that workers be given greater responsibility. Her view that creativity could flow from workers, not just managers, and that organizations had civic responsibilities to society were unique. Follett, with a background in social reform and education like Boeke's, was not taken seriously until the Hawthorne experiment confirmed her theories.

Hawthorne, the Chicago area division of Western Electric, hired consultant Elton Mayo to determine what level of lighting on its factory floor would optimize assembly line production. They expected to get higher productivity if they increased the lighting, but they wanted to know if the increases in productivity would offset the additional expense of using more electricity. Mayo completed a series of studies between 1927 and 1932 in which he first measured the pre-intervention level of productivity and then asked management to raise the level of illumination by a discernible increment. Productivity increased. He asked for another increase. Productivity increased again, and it increased each time the illumination was increased.

With the illumination rather obviously excessive, Mayo decided to double-check his results by gradually reducing it. To his amazement productivity kept going up each time he reduced illumination. When it returned to the original level, productivity was substantially higher than it had been originally. Inadvertently, Mayo had confirmed that human considerations such as management attention increased worker productivity. Lighting had little or nothing to do with it.

These findings supported Follett and launched human relations as a new professional field. In 1941 in *Dynamic Administration*, Follett asserted that delegating responsibility developed better workers. Follett also introduced the concept of "power with" rather than "power over." Peter Drucker, who created the new field of management with the publication of *The Practice of Management* in 1954, later honored Mary Parker Follett as "the prophet of management."

In the 1950s, studies in decision-making moved in both the direction of understanding human needs and toward use of more accurate data and computer simulations. Cognitive psychologist Herbert Simon received the Nobel Prize in Economics in 1978 for his studies begun in 1954 in problem solving, using computer simulations of human cognition meshed with studies in uncertainty. It is impossible, he concluded, to ever be certain because completely reliable information about the future is just not available. Simon is responsible for the term "bounded rationality" which has become a central theme in behavioral economics. It is concerned with the ways in which the decision-making process itself influences decisions. (Simon 1957)

Richard Cyert and James March also studied the messiness of real-life decision-making. In 1963 in *A Behavioral Theory of the Firm*, they presented their research that decisions made in changing and unpredictable circumstances cannot be based on predetermined, standardized rules. Decisions are actually made moment to moment based on what people have learned while working in a particular context with a particular group of people.

What Is a Decision?

As Simon, Cyert, and March all discovered, decision making is central to an organization's daily functioning. Thus, the task of governing an organization becomes one of creating an open system in which decision-making and the decision maker can adapt and function in the ever-changing environment of daily activity. To understand how Endenburg's methods solved this problem, we need to define decision-making.

A decision is actually a complex event, or many complex events with varied ramifications—a choice between alternatives. Consider a simple example: Charles arrives at the office one morning, hangs up his coat, sees a red message-waiting light blinking on his telephone. Knowing that he is prepared for his morning meeting, he decides he has enough time to get a cup of coffee before responding to the messages. He walks to the kitchen, pours his coffee, and then decides to join a conversation with two fellow workers concerning rumors about an affair between their boss and a handsome man in the Accounting Department. After a few moments, he decides to withdraw from the conversation and go back to his desk. "I've really got to stay out of such conversations," he tells himself. "They waste so much time."

In this example, Charles was the decision maker and he chose from a set of available options. Conventional theorizing about decision making might try to model Charles' range of choices or do a cost benefit study to justify having individual coffee makers put in each worker's cubicle and closing down the office kitchen altogether. A social psychologist might analyze Charles's choices in terms of interpersonal effectiveness, pointing out that Charles might rise faster in the organization if he stayed plugged into the organization's social structure.

Unlike theorists who are analyzing options, we are more interested in Charles himself as a decision maker, the *who* of decision making, if you will. In our example Charles is an autocratic decision maker, autocratic because he is an "aut-" or "auto-," a "self," mindfully making a choice among possible alternatives. Because Charles enjoyed coffee and felt a bit sleepy, he consciously chose coffee. His choice was mindful, his decision making autocratic. Under other circumstances, his decision might not have been autocratic. For example, if he had a personal belief system based on a diet book or a formal religious practice that said he should drink coffee, his decision would have been theocratic, based on a "theo-", a "god-based" or "principle-based" belief. If the workers in Charles' office had a coffee club, they might have voted on what flavor of coffee to buy next—a democratic or majority vote decision. These are all decision-making methods that we use to make decisions, to choose between alternatives.

Policy Decisions vs. Operational Decisions

Charles's first three decisions: deciding to get a cup of coffee, deciding first to join the gossip, then deciding to withdraw from the gossip were all one-time, operational decisions that Charles made as he navigated his way through what was probably his typical morning routine at the office. His fourth decision, the declaration to himself that he should generally stay away from gossipy conversations, was a personal policy decision.

A Policy Decision

A policy decision governs a set of future operational decisions by setting aims, standards, and limits. It may allocate resources, including people, clarify values, establish plans, or specify general procedures for repetitive processes.

An Operational Decision

An operational decision flows from or executes specific or implied policy decisions in the day-to-day functioning of an organization. It may determine daily job assignments, the handling of correspondence, the operation of machinery, the delivery of specific services, etc.

Defining operational and policy decisions is important because many people and organizations are not clear about the distinction or the relationship between these two kinds of decisions, leading to muddy decision-making processes and poor decisions. For example, an operational decision made to cover a unique circumstance may become a de facto policy stretched to cover all circumstances, or having made a policy decision, a manager might not follow through to see if the policy decision has been properly applied—or applied at all—in day-to-day operational decisions.

The consequences of an operational decision are usually quickly apparent because its effects are immediate. The negative effect of a policy decision, on the other hand, may not become apparent for some time. For example, Charles' policy decision not to be involved in office gossip might save time but might also affect his job. If he did not hear about his boss's affair, for example, he might subsequently make disparaging remarks about his boss' lover in her presence.

Sociocracy makes a clear distinction between these two types of decisions, policy and operational, and delegates them to different decision-making structures that we discuss more fully in the following chapters.

Integrated Policy Decision-Making

Too often organizations delegate policy decisions to the board of directors or top management that hold sporadic retreats or months of meetings with outside consultants. The resulting governance documents, often in the form of a strategic plan, may never be well understood by the rest of the organization—most of whom may never even see them.

With sociocratic governance, policy decision-making lies at the heart of the organization. This dramatically improves the efficiency of operations, the quality of production, and the development of leaders. To understand how and why Endenburg developed a structure based on inclusive, enfranchised decision-making, we need to look at the idea of power and compliance, and how they relate to consent.

Power and Compliance

The social sciences, where the management of organizations is usually studied, often define power as the ability to influence others. This definition places the source of power in charismatic leaders rather than in the organization's work. The loss of the leader would by this definition leave the organization powerless. Endenburg, as an engineer, looked instead to the physical sciences for a definition of power. Physics defines power as the ability "to perform work over time." A powerful car, for example, can reach a high speed very quickly and sustain that speed. Thinking by analogy, Endenburg designed an organization whose structure allowed it to do more work over time—a more powerful organization.

The physical sciences measure system compliance in terms of mass and physical characteristics such as resistance, friction, elasticity, and so on. With people, we also speak of resistance, friction, and elasticity but more fundamentally, in human action willingness is essential. People decide, consciously or unconsciously, whether to comply, to commit, to consistently implement agreements, or not.

Consider Charles's boss, Susan, who has decided that her staff needs to re-design their product catalog. If the staff refuses to comply with her decisions, Susan could fire them but then she would be powerless. If they were unhappy with her decision, that would produce friction. They might reduce her power by being passive or subtly sabotaging her, perhaps even by following her instructions "perfectly." Since instructions can never cover all eventualities, this resistance effectively reduces her power because less work will be accomplished.

If a high level of compliance, or commitment, builds power in organizations, how do you get compliance?

In traditional management theory, the emphasis would be on increasing Susan's ability to influence and persuade others. Endenburg knew that a powerful engine does not depend for its power on the driver. An excellent driver cannot drive a car with a flat tire as well as he can drive a car with four good tires. How then could he build strong human systems not weakened by friction and resistance?

Compliance and the Principle of Consent

A central heating system offers a good analogy for understanding consent and compliance. It consists of a furnace in the basement and a thermostat on the living room wall. The thermostat has two elements that regulate the furnace: a switch and a thermometer. The thermometer measures the temperature in the room and sends the information to the switch. The switch compares the desired and actual room temperatures and switches the furnace on or off. When switched on, the furnace produces heat—a doing function. When the thermometer, the measuring function, reports increasing room temperature, the switch evaluates this information and compares it to the desired temperature. If the temperature exceeds this target, it tells the furnace to turn off—a leadership function. Comparing feedback to criteria and issuing change orders is the basic function of leadership.

This process repeats itself as necessary to keep the house at more or less the desired temperature. The switch tells the furnace to turn on or off, the furnace does the work, and the thermometer tells the switch how the room temperature is coming along. This creates a cycle of leading-doing-measuring that we will explore later.

What if one element ignores the limitations of another? What if the switch decides the furnace, an old fashioned device designed to heat water and send it through pipes to radiators, should heat the water to 120° Celsius (about 250° Fahrenheit). If the furnace were forced to obey this autocratic decision, water would boil at 100° (212°). It would not be able to comply because the pipes would burst, the furnace would explode, and the heating system would need costly repairs.

If the switch, furnace, and thermometer decided to try traditional democracy and make decisions by majority vote, the results would not be much better. The switch and the thermometer could vote to take the temperature to 110° (230°) and the furnace could vote against it. With two votes to one, the furnace would be outnumbered. As its temperature rises past 100° (212°), it would explode again. Only by understanding that all three elements are of equal value to the operation of the system, that the compliance of each one is necessary for the functioning of the others, can they get the best result.

The analogy to human systems functioning is that if one part of the system cannot function, it "withdraws its consent," and friction and resistance increase until the system finally stops functioning. Thus, to achieve compliance from people, one must first have their consent. This concept became Endenburg's first principle for governing an organization:

The First Governing Principle

Consent governs decision-making. Consent means there are no argued and paramount objections to a proposed policy decision.

A major paradigm shift in governance and organizational thinking, this principle is based on sound science and on practical experience. Maintaining consent reduces friction and inefficiency. It maximizes creativity and productivity on the best days and prevents massive walkouts on the worst. It ensures that decisions will be made in ways that respect the needs, capabilities, and limits of all who are affected by them.

Of course, not everyone in an organization needs to consent to all decisions—nor would they want to. The principle of consent applies to those working within a domain. A domain of decision-making is *a set of activities that a decision-maker (or makers) is responsible for controlling or managing.* For example, in a sociocratically organized office, Charles would have his own personal domain in which he is able to make policy decisions without consulting others. His team's domain of decision-making would include his supervisor, Susan, and everyone she supervises. Each organizational unit in a sociocratic organization constitutes a domain and has the responsibility for pol-

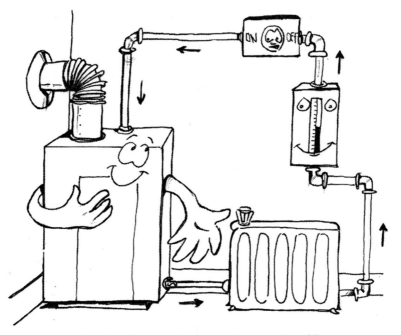

Figure 4.1 A Heating System Consents. A conventional heating system illustrates the importance of consent in decision making. Unless each element is able to function, the whole system will stop functioning.

icy decisions within its defined scope.

"Governs Decision-Making"

There are two phrases in the definition of consent decision-making that explain the rule of consent: *governs decision-making* and *no argued and paramount objections.*

In the *Declaration of Independence* of the United States we see "governments derive their just powers from the consent of the governed." The *Declaration* goes on to explain that the colonies are withdrawing their consent to participate in Great Britain's organization, the British Empire, and gives a long list of "argued and paramount objections."

Sociocratic organizations extend this same right of consent to any group of "we the people," the phrase with which the Constitution of the United States begins. They are not only allowed, they are expected to set up their own system of governance—their own constitution—and achieve consent within their area of responsibility. Policy decisions are analogous to amending the group's constitution and bylaws. A policy decision-making meeting is a group's own parliament, a round-table for making decisions as peers.

Day-to-day operational decisions, on the other hand, are not customarily made by consent. The people within a domain decide by consent how various operational decisions will be made as shown in Figure 4.2. For example, it will usually decide to have one of its members perform a leadership role and make specific decisions in an autocratic way. In some situations, like when to hold the office party, a majority vote may be appropriate and satisfactory. Religious beliefs may govern other decisions like scheduling holidays and celebrations.

The important point is that sociocratic principles require that the group make the fundamental policy decisions by consent. By consent, they decide on the use of majority vote, autocratic leadership, chaos, solidarity, etc. Consent is thus the first principle of governance and underlies all other decisions. People must consent to work together and may withdraw their consent as circumstances change.

In sociocratic organizations, there is an option to consent to use consensus. Definitions of consensus vary. In some cases, consensus means that participants must agree to say "yes" to a proposal with a level of commitment that is close to solidarity (Boeke 1945). In other cases, it means only that they agree that this is the best agreement that can be found (Avery 1981; Butler 1987; Dressler 2006; Susskind and Cruikshank 2006). In the later case, the definition of and use of consensus is very close to the use of consent in sociocracy. A distinction is that consent in sociocracy is used in the context of a governance structure that applies consent decision-making methodically to all policy decisions. This governance structure also ensures a process for regular measurement and evaluation of the effectiveness of consensus decisions.

There is also the option in sociocracy to consent to chaos. Chaos is not random nor is it uncontrolled. Random activity is totally chance and true random activity is probably not possible among normally functioning humans.

Chaos, as Prigogine discovered, means having many possibilities. There is great potential energy in chaos. Chaotic conditions will self-organize only if two conditions are present: a source of energy and equivalence of the elements. For example, if someone yells, "Fire! Over there!" in a crowd at a county fair, the crowd may immediately self-organize a bucket brigade to put out the fire. If a favored politician appears, the crowd will form a line to shake hands. All these possibili-

Decision-Making Methods
Used in Sociocratic Organizations

For Policy Decisions:
   Consent (No Argued and Paramount Objections)

For Day-to-Day Operational Decisions:
   Chaos ("Everyone go for it!")
   Theocratic, Ideological, Magical, or other Belief Systems
   Autocratic or Authoritarian
   Majority Vote
   Consensus
   Solidarity

Figure 4.2 Decision-making Methods Used in Sociocratic Organizations. Consent is used for policy decisions, which are analogous to constitutional or bylaws decisions. The circle, the decision-making group, by consent, then determines what methods are most appropriate for making day-to-day operational decisions.

ties are present in a chaotic crowd. It can immediately self-organize in unpredictable ways.

The circle is structured for self-organizing. The aim is the source of energy and the principle of consent creates equivalence. Consent decision-making can thus trigger the self-organizing characteristic of chaos to support creativity and efficiency. In doing so, consent decision-making thus gives us the ability to guide, or "steer," our organizations in changing, even chaotic conditions.

A typical sociocratic organization spends a relatively small percentage of its time in consent decision-making. Most of the time, it governs itself using whatever methods seem most efficient. Consent still governs decision making, however, because the "citizens" of the organization can withdraw their consent—for argued and paramount reasons.

"Argued and Paramount Objections"

The second key phrase in the rule of consent decision-making is *argued and paramount objections*. Endenburg developed the sociocratic method using the language and concepts that engineers use, namely, mathematical terms, and sociocracy continues to rely on the engineering meanings of some words. One of those words is *argument*. *Argument* does not mean "a loud and violent expression of feeling that rarely leads to a good resolution." Rather it means "the clear expression of a truth or of a characteristic." A glass of water has arguments, i.e. physical attributes that can be expressed precisely in mathematical language. You cannot stick your hand through the side of a glass of water; some of its arguments (i.e. hardness) prevent it. However, you can stick your hand over the rim into the water because H2O has different arguments. Your car consents to be driven wherever you please, but withdraws its consent by showing a red light on the dashboard arguing that low oil pressure prevents it.

An argument as used in formal logic refers both to statements of fact and to the conclusions drawn from them. For example, "A equals B" and "B equals C" are statements of fact. "Therefore A equals C" is a conclusion drawn from these facts. Thus in sociocracy, arguments include both statements of fact and conclusions drawn from them.

This does not mean that an argument has to be stated as one might if one were a philosopher of logic or a theoretical mathematician. It only means that an objection must be presented clearly enough for others to understand and address it. An objection that cannot be understood cannot be resolved. An objection may start out as a niggle or a vaguely unpleasant feeling, and in this sense, a niggle would be acceptable as a beginning argument, although other members of the circle would have to explore the feeling to understand the objection and resolve it.

What makes an objection *paramount*? As we saw in the example of the furnace, a system's parts must always remain within their defined limits. These limits in human terms may be more flexible than in mechanical systems but those limits still exist. When a system, mechanical or human, moves outside its limits, it will no longer be able to function. An objection is paramount if it is based on a factor or factors whose arguments are outside the limits of the system. *Paramount* means "above all others, of chief concern or importance."

A person who is able to keep her equilibrium with a wide variety of people and in many delicate social situations has wider limits than a person who requires a more predictable work environment.

Thus, a paramount objection is one that is determined by the range of one's limits. A typical paramount objection might begin with "I object because I won't be able to do my job for the following reasons...."

An argued and paramount objection is thus a statement that a person's paramount needs or concerns would be negatively affected by the proposed decision. It says, "Some aspect of me is in danger of going out of safe limits or will be unable to perform as required if this proposal is implemented." In a sociocratically governed organization it is important that every human and nonhuman part of the organization's systems be able to express this inability to function and to be heard. Once these objections are resolved, the organization can move forward much more smoothly and effectively than an organization that tries to ignore friction or override resistance.

As we saw in our example of the central-heating system, although a switch may be delicate, the thermometer sensitive, and the furnace expensive, if the system is to produce heat each element is equally important. Each is powerless without the other. They must resolve any and all paramount and argued objections for the whole to function optimally.

The requirement to resolve objections transforms decision making from a struggle for control into a process of puzzle solving.

Reason, Not Veto

The principle of consent is not about the right of veto but about the right to argue. Everyone has the right—and even the obligation—to raise argued and paramount objections to a proposal. Objections are useful and a good meeting facilitator will seek them out. For example, if a person says "no objection" during a consent round but has a downcast look and her arms folded, the facilitator might tactfully inquire to determine whether she was in fact troubled by something about the proposal.

Consent is an inescapable precondition of organizational behavior. Sociocratic organizations establish consent consciously with specific procedures. They do not wait until a worker is in exit interview before they find out what the worker thinks about the organization. When we realize that paramount objections are important to the continued functioning of the organization, it becomes clear that the principle of consent and recognition of everyone's equal value is an extremely practical way of addressing resources and abilities.

The prevailing form of decision-making will determine human behavior. If an authoritarian system prevails, behavior will include both stagnant compliance and passive aggressiveness. When majority rule prevails, there will be divisiveness and manipulation of votes. When consent decision-making prevails, people and organizations flourish.

CHAPTER FIVE

Developing Quality

❦

To understand why sociocracy offers superior quality in products and services, it is helpful to take a historical perspective. Work as we know it developed in artisan workshops where the master craftsman determined quality and was the sole arbiter of acceptable work. Through the apprenticeship system that started for boys at the age of fourteen, and sometimes younger, the artisans controlled both training and production and ensured quality through direct supervision. Often, the workshops were attached to the home and the apprentices lived with the master.

The role of the artisan in controlling quality began to decline as early as the 1300s when large industrial organizations began to emerge (Tuchman 1978) and culminated in Fordism in 1910 with the de-skilling of assembly line production using minimally-trained factory workers. Approaches to quality began to change in the 1920s with Mary Parker Follet advocating more worker participation in management decisions. The Hawthorne experiment of the 1930s encouraged companies to find ways to involve workers in planning and to use their creativity not only to increase productivity but to improve quality. This new approach proved to be not only more humane but more profitable.

The focus of quality management moved to the markets. Since the artisan, the former arbiter of quality and taste and the provider of worker education, no longer defined quality or provided education, the customer or client became the measure of quality. The intended client was the judge that mattered. Quality was what the customer said it was.

With the explosion in new materials and manufacturing methods, however, the customers found themselves not always able to evaluate new products. Things broke, poisoned the users, and were often incompatible with other products. With increased specialization, business-to-business services grew and businesses themselves became the unhappy customers in the new climate of dubious quality control. Rapidly increasing mobility meant that businesses as well as customers were "here today and gone tomorrow." With globalization, businesses and customers were geographically separated and often did not speak the same language. International standards became necessary not only to ensure quality but to protect businesses from businesses.

Quality Standards

Some readers may remember when "Made in Japan" meant "junk." Thanks to Edward Deming, Joseph Juran, and a lot of hard work by the Japanese, by the 1970s "Made in Japan" meant high quality and low cost. Japanese products flooded the American market and sent business leaders into shock. The economic success of such superior Japanese products spurred broad awareness of the importance of quality in Western markets.

Deming worked as a statistician and physicist teaching in universities and consulting to corporations in America and abroad on ways to improve quality through statistical analysis. His method is known as Total Quality Management (TQM). Juran's contribution to quality management was adding a human dimension to quality—broadening it from its statistical origins. In 1937, Juran conceptualized the Pareto Principle to help separate the "vital few" from the "useful many" in their activities. This is commonly referred to as the 80-20 principle and its universal application makes it one of the most useful concepts and tools in modern organizations. His classic work, *Managerial Breakthrough* (1964) was the first to describe a step-by-step sequence for improving the quality of goods and services. This process has evolved into Six Sigma and is the basis for quality initiatives worldwide.

Juran describes quality from the customer's perspective as having two aspects. First, higher quality means a greater number of features that meet customers' needs. Second, it means "freedom from trouble," meaning higher quality consists of fewer defects.

Today, the most widely recognized standard of quality is the International Organization for Standardization (ISO). Begun in 1947 with delegates from 25 countries, ISO is now a consortium of 148 national standards institutes, one from each participating country. Because this name when translated into many languages produces many acronyms, the organization has adopted the standard acronym of ISO from the Greek *isos* meaning "equal."

ISO representatives establish specifications and criteria for the classification of materials, the manufacture and supply of products, testing and analysis, terminology, and the provision of services. This standard framework, a common technological language, facilitates trade and the transfer of technology world-wide.

In Europe, where sociocratic principles and methods were developed, ISO 9000 certification is crucial. An ISO 9000 certified organization is one that has consistently demonstrated an ability to provide products and services that enhance customer or client satisfaction and meet applicable regulatory requirements. The certification process is rigorous. An organization is at a big disadvantage if it is not ISO 9000 certified.

ISO 9000, originating in 1987 and updated several times, is concerned with management quality, what the organization does to continually enhance customer or client satisfaction while at the same time meeting or exceeding industry regulations and requirements. While the vast majority of ISO standards are specific to a particular product, material, or process and thus apply only to one industry, ISO 9000 is applicable to the management of all organizations—businesses, governments, and associations. It is the most widely used of the ISO standards and is rapidly becoming world-wide the minimum standard for quality in business management that it has become in Europe.

This emphasis on quality comes at a price, however. Many a business executive has groaned over the expense of these certifications in time and money spent on paperwork, document preparation, and payments to consultants. And more than one has cursed the process as an exercise in "baloney," snickering when told that a company went out of business possibly due to the expense of their quality control systems after receiving the most prestigious annual award, the Malcolm Baldrige National Quality Award sponsored by the National Institute of Standards and Technology (NIST). A quality system can become a "quality albatross."

To receive ISO certification, companies hire registrars, independent of the ISO, to conduct "conformity assessments." These regulators validate whether the products, materials, services, systems, and people in a particular organization meet the relevant ISO standards. But even before hiring regulators, companies hire consultants to examine their companies and send their managers to educational programs that teach them to do readiness audits, pre-assessment audits, document writing and review, internal auditor training, employee training,

Figure 5.1 A Circle Meeting. Everyone in a sociocratic organization is a member of a circle that governs their day-to-day work. Circle members function as peers when deciding how their aims will be accomplished.

and implementation planning.

The mixed message of quality and performance accentuates the remarkable nature of the experience of ISO and sociocracy. Endenburg Electrotechniek was able to receive ISO 9000 certification in about a year *with none of the extensive preparation usually required for the certification audit.* With the help of Roland Angenent, then a doctoral student, all the Endenburg Electrotechniek workers had to do was review the standards and compile the relevant reports from their logbooks. Along with completing some additional forms, much of this work was translating documents into ISO-acceptable terminology. They did not have to hire outside consultants, undertake special training, or set aside time for pre-audit audits. They were already working according to quality principles.

The Circle

Quality in a sociocratic organization is ensured by the structure of interlinked circles that governs the organization. This circle structure reflects the operational structure and sets the policies that determine how the organization will provide services or meet production quotas on a day-to-day basis.

The Second Governing Principle

A circle is a semi-autonomous and self-organizing unit that has its own aim. It makes policy decisions within its domain; delegates the leading, doing, and measuring functions to its own members; maintains its own memory system; and plans its own development.

Traditional autocratic organizations assign policy decisions to the board of directors and top management, but in sociocratic organizations, each member belongs to at least one circle and participates in making the policy decisions that govern their day-to-day work. An individual circle includes everyone working within a domain, a defined sphere of responsibility. This circle determines the policies governing that domain. Circles normally range from one to forty people, including managers, supervisors, heads, chairs, workers, staff, volunteers, etc., and meet on a regular basis at least every four to six weeks.

Returning to our earlier example, Charles, with his co-workers

Abdul, Bonnie, and Susan, have a common aim to provide communication services about their company's technology and are organizing a technical conference. Their company operates sociocratically. Their circle meets on the first Monday of every month. Six months ago they selected Susan as their circle meeting facilitator and Charles as their secretary, both for one year terms. As secretary, Charles schedules meetings, takes notes, and sends out minutes. At the last month's meeting the circle decided the agenda for this meeting would include an evaluation of their recent users conference and a review of changes they might need in their policies or strategies for organizing the next conference.

Each member has a copy of the logbook that serves as the memory of the circle. Since Charles is secretary of a small circle, he also serves as logbook keeper. The secretary or logbook keeper is responsible for ensuring that the logbooks are up-to-date. These books give each member a record of the circle's history and the current decisions concerning its work processes and aims.

A circle's responsibility encompasses all the activities associated with accomplishing its aim. All the functions of leading-doing-measuring are under the control of the circle. It is responsible for both producing its organization and organizing its production, meaning that it decides how to use its members and resources in order to create and deliver its products or services. Circle meetings make all the policy decisions related to these topics.

In traditional autocratic organizations, the majority of members only attend staff meetings that focus almost exclusively on the production process, the doing. They do not ordinarily participate in policy discussions or determination. In sociocratic organizations all members participate in both kinds of meetings, although there are likely to be far fewer staff meetings because circle meetings give clear guidance and delegate work very effectively. Because all workers can participate in circle meetings they are less likely to need as much supervision.

At the risk of repetition, sociocracy assigns policy determination and policy execution activities to every level of the organization. In autocratically structured organizations, the "top" determines the policy and leaves the execution to the "bottom." In sociocracy each circle determines and executes its own policy within the limits that have been set, with its consent, by the larger organization.

Typical Topics for a Circle Meeting

Vision, mission, and aim

Policy and strategy plans

Progress of the circle toward its aim

Design of work processes

Circle's organizational design and procedures that flow from it

Function and task descriptions of circle members

Election of circle members to functions and tasks

Removal of someone from the circle

The circle's development plan

Figure 5.2 Typical Topics for a Circle Meeting. Circle meetings discuss any subject that affects the work of the circle but focus on those topics related to "leading" including planning, scheduling, assessing, and setting criteria. Unlike staff meetings that focus on daily operational decisions, circle meetings focus on policy decisions.

Creating Organization: The Organization of Work

A circle's fundamental responsibility is to realize its aim. It executes that responsibility by organizing itself in such a way that it will accomplish all its required tasks. Figure 5.3 illustrates the steps required in creating organization: defining the vision, mission, and aim; designing a production process and a circular process; designing task division and delegation; and designing a program of task delegation. These steps are presented sequentially but they may occur simultaneously. The clearest starting place is often to define an aim because it most closely relates to the purpose and daily concerns of the members of the circle. Vision and mission are more abstract and the production process is more concrete.

Vision

A vision is a description of the future as the circle desires it to be. It is a dream of how wonderful the world would become if the organization could fulfill its aims. The image may include conditions, feelings, and values. It is typically external in that it defines the world outside the organization, the one that could be created as a result of the organization's work.

In our example, the vision of Charles' circle is that all the company's clients will be fully informed and excited about the company's products.

Mission

A mission, closely related to "missionary," is a statement of the circle's overall approach to realizing its vision. It is what motivates the members of the circle and reflects the circle's particular relationship to the client or to the larger organization. Where the vision defines the desired external world, the mission looks inward and defines the circle's responsibility in relation to that vision.

The mission of Charles' circle, for example, is to communicate with the company's clients through all effective media channels about the company's products and to customize that information to the clients' interests.

Aim

An aim describes an intended result, a product, or service. It is tangible and can be delivered and received. Clients must be able to recognize the aim and to differentiate it from other aims, other products or services. In fact, the circle should define its aim from the point of view of the client. In terms of quality, it encapsulates Juran's concept that quality is something that meets client's needs and has fewer defects than other products. The aim breathes practical life into the relationship with the client.

This year the aim of Charles' circle, for example, is to organize user conferences, write monthly interactive newsletters, administer user online forums, and run an outstanding user recognition program for innovative users of the company's products.

The aim is a yardstick for measuring success and a basis on which to evaluate arguments for or against decisions. Only with a well-defined aim can the circle judge the validity of paramount and reasoned arguments. A clear, well-formulated aim is necessary to prevent us from talking (and working) at cross-purposes and is a prerequisite for proper steering in an ever-changing environment. The aim is a fundamental concept that we will explore in more detail in Chapter 12, "Organizing Work."

The Production Process

An aim is the jumping off point for designing the concrete production process, the "doing." Once a circle has defined its aim, it next designs the steps it will take to produce the product(s) or service envisioned in the aim.

How should a circle organize its work? Let's look more closely at doing. Cybernetically speaking, doing has three phases. In formal systems language, these three phases are: input, transformation, and output. Translated into everyday language: the circle makes an agreement or contract with their client (input), creates the product or service (transformation), and obtains client acceptance (output).

In the case of Charles' conference the agreement phase (input) would begin with a proposal for a conference based on the needs of potential conference registrants. "Creating the service," the second phase (transformation), would be producing the conference itself, and client acceptance might be measured primarily through evaluation forms and sales made as a result of the conference.

Designing the production process, combined with the next step, designing a steering process, are what gives a sociocratic organization many advantages in quality control. Supported by the other steps, these two steps, design of production and steering processes, are the core of what we mean by creating organization.

Creating Organization

Define a Vision
Define a Mission
Define an Aim
Design a Production Process
Design a Circular Process
Determine Task Division and Delegation
Design a Program of Ongoing Development

Figure 5.3 Creating Organization. The steps in creating an organization that supports the work process generally begin with the aim, rather than the vision, because aims are often easier to define. Other steps may be done in order but may also require working back and forth revising each one until the process is complete.

The Circular Process

The circle organizes itself to function dynamically by including "measuring" and "leading" along with "doing" as part of its own work. This dynamic quality, as we will discuss more fully later, is the result of building feedback processes into the circle's organization. The circle is thus not only responsible for doing its work, it is responsible for measuring and for evaluating its own work. This process of leading-doing-measuring incorporates a "feedback loop" into the work process and is essential to correcting and improving the circle's product or service. This circular process is illustrated in Figure 5.4.

The reason for including all the steps of the circular process within one circle, rather than separating it out between various departments or people as traditional autocratically structured organizations often do, is that each circle member is then prepared to handle the inevitable disturbances of the real world workplace. If nothing unpredictable occurred, the production processes would never need to change, but this is impossible. A well-constructed leading-doing-measuring process that everyone in the circle understands means that the circle members can correct their own work on a moment-to-moment basis.

It is possible to supplement the circular process functions by creating specialized departments (personnel, accounting, research, and development, etc.) but primary responsibility for leading-doing-measuring is within the circle, in the hands of the *socius*, the associates.

For example, Charles' circle has written instructions for each step needed to prepare and run a conference, from budgeting for the conference and developing conference themes, to publicizing and running it, to collecting and analyzing feedback forms and sales figures. Each doing step then has its own circular process for leading-doing-measuring. The measurements may produce results that lead to changes in the instructions.

Task Division and Delegation

The circle allocates primary functions and tasks to its members. For daily tasks, the circle may decide to give the operations leader the responsibility for allocating work autocratically. For other tasks, workers might draw straws, vote, or rotate responsibilities. But in all instances the circle as a whole decides by consent which process will

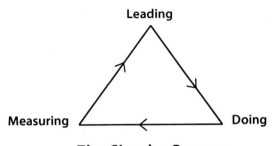

The Circular Process

Figure 5.4 The Circular Process. The circular process is illustrated as a triangle. The sides of the triangle represent the lines of communication between functions. This triangle, often used to represent the circle as well, has become the symbol of sociocracy.

be used and who will be responsible for executing it.

Development

A circle is more than a list of people assigned to a set of tasks. It is a semi-autonomous, self-organizing, organic entity that is capable of responding to its environment as it continues to function in accordance with accomplishing its aim. It changes according to need. To do this it must be continually developing. This requires researching, learning, and teaching. A circle organizes these activities for itself and consciously controls its own development.

The importance of including development as one of the responsibilities of the circle became clear in 1979 when another of many outside researchers visited Endenburg Electrotechniek to study the results of implementing sociocracy. This study revealed that at the departmental level, after nine years of operation, people were not participating in the governance process. Circle meetings were not just poorly attended, some were not being held.

What this study revealed is that more was required for people to participate in governance than just informing them of the opportunity. Endenburg realized that people who had worked in organizations with implicitly or explicitly autocratic leadership needed to "undergo a phase of complete democratization before converting to sociocracy." (Endenburg 1998) In other words, they needed to have the experience of participating in governance before they could take full responsibility for governing themselves.

Endenburg decided to do a second implementation of sociocracy and make circles responsible for their own development—their own learning, teaching, and research.

The term "learning organization" is familiar to many but, in practical terms, not particularly well defined. Peter Senge's classic work, *The Fifth Discipline: The Art and Practice of The Learning Organization* (1990), defines the learning attitude, the benefits of the learning frame of mind, and the importance of learning for organizations. He advocates an attitude of openness to learning and describes the benefits it should produce.

Sociocracy agrees with Senge's ideas for the learning organization; both are based on systems thinking and an understanding of the importance of steering processes and adjustment to change in order to develop and to remain competitive. Sociocracy expands this concept of development to include teaching others and researching aspects of the circle's work to develop new methods and concepts. Development —learning, teaching, and research—is central to planning the circle's work and work expectations.

The circle and circle members determine the direction of development in their responsibility area, choosing new processes and products, and responding to changing needs.

Why Design Organizations This Way?

In addition to addressing the issues of quality in production and services, organizing work sociocratically brings numerous benefits because:

- Complex processes remain steerable.
- Processes do not become isolated from their environment.
- Circle members understand their domain (their common aim and process).
- Circle members are responsible for the results of their circle.
- No gaps occur between processes.
- Each process, on every level in the organization, follows the same general system, greatly simplifying problem-solving.
- The management and/or information system is integral to the

primary work process.

- Orientation towards the client is included in the process.

Sociocracy can be applied in medical practices, scrabble clubs, summer camps, automotive factories, schools, sporting events, theater productions, and associations of all kinds. In this sense it is often referred to as an "empty tool." Each organization fills in its own content. Some problems that appear to be content problems may in fact be solved by adjusting the "empty form."

The process for designing a sociocratic organization, the design of dynamic governance, is always the same, for groups or individuals—only the content changes. This is one of the beauties of learning sociocratic principles and methods. It works universally. It is more like understanding organization rather than learning a specific way of organizing.

CHAPTER SIX

Steering & Structure

❦

In physics, an element that is changing is referred to as *dynamic*. Thus, a dynamic environment is one that is unstable, or capable of change, as opposed to being static, or incapable of change. Since our natural environment is dynamic, our most effective organizations will be those that are dynamic as well, those that can change in response to both internal and external changes, whether they are pressures or opportunities, adapting in much the same way a living organism adapts.

Sociocratic organizations are dynamic by design. To optimize the advantages of responsiveness and reduce the disadvantages of instability, they use the circular process of leading-doing-measuring to steer their work. This enables them to adjust and adapt quickly and efficiently while maintaining control over their processes. The circular process builds positive and negative feedback and anticipatory feed-forward loops into both decision-making and production. By ensuring that every cycle of work returns information that must be evaluated while leading the next cycle, sociocratically governed organizations ensure that their functioning will remain dynamic at all levels.

Double-Linking

In addition to embedding feedback and feed-forward loops into the work process, sociocracy embeds them into its governance structure. As we have seen, the sociocratic governance structure extends throughout the organization in a series of circles that correspond to departments and teams, or areas of interest and responsibility. Within these circles, all work processes are designed to establish and maintain the circular process of leading-doing-measuring. The circular process is maintained between circles by double-links.

The Third Governing Principle

The connection between two circles is a double-link formed by the operational leader and one or more representatives who participate fully in the decision making of the next higher circle.

This third principle, called double-linking, is unique to sociocracy. As illustrated in Figure 6.1, circles, the policy-making units that govern work units, are linked by at least two people who provide direction (a leading function) and feedback (a measuring function) between the circles. This design establishes and maintains a dynamic process that keeps the whole organization responsive and open to change.

Circle A selects the operational leader of Circle B, for example, the

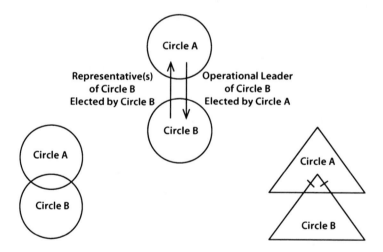

Figure 6.1 Double Links Between Circles. Double links maintain feedback and feed-forward loops between circles to enable circular processes. The operational leader is responsible for communicating the needs of Circle A to Circle B. The representative(s) of Circle B are responsible for communicating the needs of Circle B to Circle A. To show that both links participate fully in both circles, the circles are shown overlapping. The traditional way of drawing "krings" uses triangles to illustrate the upward and downward movement of communications with hash marks to indicate the links.

supervisor of a production unit or the chair of a working committee. Circle B would select one or more representatives to Circle A. The operational leader carries information down the organization. The representative(s) carry information up the organization.

Following our example of Charles, who works in a software development company, Circle A might be the Marketing Department Circle and Circle B the Publicity Unit Circle where Charles works. Susan is the operational leader of the Publicity Unit Circle and carries information from the Marketing Department Circle to the Publicity Unit Circle. When the Publicity Unit Circle elects Charles to be their representative, he carries information from the Publicity Unit Circle to the Marketing Department Circle, completing the circular process.

Representatives should have an ability to communicate the concerns of their circle members to the next higher circle, as well as an ability to think at the next higher level of abstraction. The operational leader, on the other hand, is responsible for directing the lower circle and communicating the needs of the organization to that circle. These two roles cannot be assigned to one person because leading and measuring must operate separately and simultaneously. Using an analogy to electricity, power cannot flow in two directions at once on one wire.

Both links participate fully in Circle A and Circle B and are present when the other link is selected. Thus, the representative from Circle B is present in Circle A when the operational leader is selected and must consent, and the operational leader selected by Circle A is participating in Circle B when it selects its representatives to Circle A and must consent. To understand the importance of double-linking we need to understand how the circular process maintains positive and negative feedback and anticipatory feed-forward loops.

Circular Processes

In any process, if feedback is absent or ignored, changes will be random or, at best, made on the basis of incomplete information. It is feedback that tells us whether we are doing well or poorly. Evaluating and acting on feedback allows us to improve or change our behavior. To design a good system of feedback we need to determine what we need to know and when we need to know it. In our earlier example of the heating system, the necessary feedback was temperature. Like the gauges on the panel of an airplane, feedback signals the system when something is not working or needs to be adjusted.

The leading-doing-measuring loop is a circular process that steers a system by telling it when to start, stop, or change. The thermostat in the heating system that we discussed earlier is one part of the circular process that provides feedback to the switch so it can "know" when to turn the furnace on or off.

In autocratic governance structures, those in charge, the bosses, can ignore feedback. In sociocratic structures, they cannot. The principle of consent, the first governing principle, ensures that feedback cannot be ignored *within* circles; double-linking, the third governing principle, ensures that feedback cannot be ignored *between* circles. Feedback, an essential element of the circular process of leading-doing-measuring is essential to steering in a dynamic environment.

Types of Steering

As shown in Figure 6.2 steering can be *passive* or *active*, and *static* or *dynamic*. Each is effective in a different circumstances. Passive steering simply reacts to the environment while active steering attempts to change in anticipation of the environment. Static steering requires no internal changes, while dynamic steering fully utilizes the leading-doing-measuring cycle, the circular process, to make both the internal and external changes necessary to remain viable.

For example, a turtle pulling into its shell is using passive-static steering to protect itself from a threat in the environment. Since turtles have been acting this way for millions of years, it is quite effective for them. A school system that simply limits enrollments when classes are overcrowded is using passive-static steering as well, but it may not be so effective for the community.

A textile mill that asks the government to erect trade barriers to keep out foreign competition is asking for support for passive static steering in the form of protective legislation. Organizations that use passive static steering set up barriers between themselves and the problem without interacting with the threatening force or making changes internally. In the long run, experience has shown that building barriers damages organizations and economies.

Organizations using active static steering respond to their environments by seeking a new non-threatening environment. A rabbit uses speed to move to a new environment where there is no threatening fox. A school system buses children from overcrowded school buildings to a neighboring school system. A clothing company lowers its costs by building factories in another country where labor is less expensive. Actions are taken but the system doesn't change; it escapes.

In dynamic steering, on the other hand, the circular process is used to change the system, not just react to the environment. Passive dynamic steering is a *difference-controlled process* that measures any difference between current conditions and an established norm or criterion. The difference becomes the basis for making any needed correction.

The heating system cited earlier uses passive dynamic or difference-controlled steering. The desired temperature is set and the switch turns the furnace on when the room temperature falls below the set temperature. The typical inventory system also uses difference-controlled steering. When stocks of supplies fall below a set point, an inventory clerk or a computer will initiate an order for more. A school board that decides to build more classroom buildings when its current classrooms reach a specified level of overcrowding is also using passive dynamic, difference-controlled steering.

Difference-controlled steering is relatively simple but it can result in relatively large fluctuations due to lag times. If the temperature outside drops sharply, it may take a while for the furnace to get the room

TYPES OF STEERING

	STATIC	DYNAMIC
PASSIVE	**Hide** Hunker Down Limit school enrollments.	**Respond** Respond to Events If classrooms are crowded, build more.
ACTIVE	**Escape** Run Away Bus children elsewhere.	**Anticipate** Forecast Events Track births and housing starts, then build classrooms in anticipation of overcrowding.

Figure 6.2 **Types of Steering.** Static organizations react to their environments and use static steering methods. Dynamic organizations interact with their environments by using circular processes to build feedback and feed-forward loops that anticipate and respond to future conditions.

warmed. If the school board starts building new classrooms only when overcrowding starts to occur, students may experience severe overcrowding before new classrooms are ready. A business using only difference-controlled or passive dynamic steering might be bankrupt before a significant change could be corrected.

So while passive dynamic steering is more adaptive than passive static steering, it is not as adaptive as it could be if it measured the factors that *cause* the need to change, *cause-controlled steering*.

In addition to feed*back* loops, systems based on cause-controlled steering use feed-*forward* loops to make forecasts of the future. They create projections or models of the system and how future events might affect it. Our heating system, for example, would have been cause-controlled if it had a thermometer on the outside of the building that measured outdoor air changes and could trigger the furnace to begin or stop warming in anticipation of environmental changes that would soon affect room temperatures. This kind of steering would use a systems model that included both the thermal conductivity of the walls (R value) and the heat output of the furnace. This information would let the switch calculate how fast the temperature in the room would fall when the temperatures outside changed. It would know when to turn on the furnace to prevent a temperature drop inside the house or to turn it off to prevent over-warming when the sun rose. This system would greatly reduce temperature fluctuations inside the house producing a more harmonious environment.

A school board that watches births and forecasts of housing starts and regional economic development to predict when it will need to build new classrooms is using active dynamic steering. Active dynamic steering allows a company to predict future demand and make innovations in its products to anticipate that demand.

The system models required for active dynamic steering can be very complex and require extensive computer programming to establish and monitor them. With the heating system, for example, the thermal conductivity of the walls might vary depending on wind speed and direction, barometric pressure, and humidity. Sensors could be installed to measure these environmental conditions and feed data to an artificial intelligence program that would help the switch "learn" the effects of its on-off decisions, given these variables. Over time it would self-correct and become more sensitive and accurate. An even more sophisticated heating system could improve its own components as new technology became available, as different people occupied the room, and as climatic conditions changed, for example, to require air cooling in addition to heating.

Feedback and Feed-Forward Loops

When organizations begin to use the circular process, specifically active dynamic, cause-controlled steering, performance improves significantly. They take more variables into account, anticipate external changes more accurately, and make internal changes more effectively. For example, in Charles' circle they try to anticipate what users will be interested in during the next conference, which may be months away. They make written predictions, plan around them, update their predictions as they get new information, and revise their plan accordingly.

The drawback of anticipatory feed-forward loops, and thus of active dynamic steering, is that predicting the future cannot be completely accurate. Models or assumptions about the environment and other variable factors are only as good as the predictions. Feed-forward loops can dampen most fluctuations, unpredictable variables, but we can't trust that they will always keep a system within tolerable limits. For example, the school board that anticipates an influx of children might fail to anticipate an economic downturn that depopulates the town of young families.

Thus an organization needs both feedback and feed-forward steering. In practical terms, circle meetings should focus both measuring current conditions as well as anticipating change and what it means for their prediction model.

Static vs. Dynamic Governance Structures

Double-links are vital in creating an organization that is at least passively dynamic. Representatives need to be able to give feedback to members of other circles about the needs of their own circle. Operational leaders need to give guidance to their circle about the needs of the larger organization.

As discussed earlier, static governance is by nature autocratic. It is linear. The leader determines policy, establishes strategies, and passes them along to the other end of the line. The linear governance and leadership structure is a very powerful way to direct "doing." Military organizations use linear command structures in training soldiers to follow orders exactly and quickly. These structures are also static and unchanging. They work well when no ambiguity can be tolerated. Their aim is to create strong forces of people who can function under the worst conditions and still maintain strong bonds and allegiances to their aim. This works well when the task, however difficult and dangerous, is well defined and can be executed quickly.

A static, linear structure, however, cannot respond well to change because it has no feedback loops. Traditionally, soldiers are not often invited to share their opinions and are even less often expected to volunteer them. You don't see a time-out called in the midst of a riot so police officers can discuss strategy. They have an aim and are pledged to fulfill it using a pre-determined set of techniques, to follow orders.

In linear structures, an action is conceived at one end "of the line" and executed on the other. Like the force that propels a bullet from a gun, however, energy created at one end of a trajectory dissipates as it travels toward the other end. According to the laws of thermodynamics, this is because energy transforms in only one direction—from a usable form to an unusable form. It has no ability to renew itself. This inevitable movement toward dissipation is the negative quality of the linear leadership structure. In complex organizations where an order must be implemented several levels away, this dissipation factor deeply undermines the positive quality of being able to precisely direct and control action. In linear structures, energy must be constantly renewed from the top. The commander can never sleep.

Figure 6.3 The Heavy Load of Autocratic Management.
When all decisions are pushed to the top, managers feel the burden of the organization on their shoulders.

This burden is why the autocratic leadership structure is like a ball and chain to virtually everyone in our complex modern organizations. The disintegration in clarity that inevitably occurs as soon as an autocratic leader attempts to transmit a policy to the doers forces the doers to continually return for clarification. As they stray from what the leader intends, the leader must exert more effort to monitor their activities. As shown in Figure 6.3, a static, autocratic, linear structure creates a constant pressure on leaders to inspire, motivate, make more decisions, and correct more actions.

As in Fordism, the more leaders in an autocratic system respond to requests for decisions and guidelines, the more they tend to "de-skill" jobs, centralize leadership functions, and create an organization that cannot respond to change.

Sociocratic structures avoid this ossification at the bottom and the burn-out at the top by involving everyone in steering the organization toward its aim. The structure is the network of double-linked circles. It integrates the negative and positive feedback and anticipatory feed-forward loops into the work process, creating active, dynamic, cause-controlled steering at all levels of the organization. This structure ensures that energy travels "up" as well as "down."

Feedback does occur, of course, in autocratic linear organizations, but it is informal, undependable, uneven, and very easily ignored. It varies according to "who has the boss's ear this week." This informal feedback can also be ignored if the boss doesn't like it or chooses not to believe it. There is no requirement that it even be acknowledged.

Some leaders in autocratically structured companies have tried to correct this feedback problem. In one socially conscious company, the president steps away from his desk for two weeks a year to have a conversation with each one of the 200 people in his company. Other organizations hold meetings similar to town meetings. But this kind of feedback is not hard-wired into the formal structure of the organization. It is not part of the work process. It is still focused on the leader and subject to one person's ability to listen and evaluate accurately.

In addition, with the focus on the autocratic leader instead of on the organization's steering or on its circular processes, feedback is often unfairly focused on the personality or skills of the leader instead of on the systems within which the leader works. The leader is thus often credited with the success or the failure of a whole company. In a sociocratic organization the successes, and failures, are shared more equitably.

Double-Linking & Dynamic Governance

As we discussed in relation to consent, the concept of hierarchy has negative connotations for many people because they equate *hierarchy* with *autocracy*, specifically with the static autocratic governance structure of most organizations. This has obscured the importance of the hierarchy in the organization of work. In a dynamic sociocratic hierarchy, there is authority associated with either the "top down" or the "bottom up" structure. No person has power over another without that person's consent. Sociocratic organizations build "power with" rather than "power over."

Further, the autocratic hierarchy obscures the importance of identifying and locating the levels of abstraction in work. (Jacques 1996) The "lower" levels of work tend to have shorter time frames and are less abstract. The "higher" levels are more abstract and concerned with longer time frames. The higher levels are generally more concerned with issues that affect several circles, rather than tasks that might concern only one circle. In Charles' company, for example, his Publicity Unit Circle is concerned with a specific area, communication with clients about the company's products. The next higher circle, the Marketing Department Circle, looks at broader issues related to communications, image, advertising, etc. Two members of Charles' circle, Susan as the operational leader and Charles as the representative, would participate in the Marketing Department Circle and the decisions made there, but the specific decisions about communications with clients are made in Charles' circle.

While the Marketing Circle is concerned with marketing, the next higher circle, the General Circle, looks at issues that affect the work of all the circles. The General Circle is responsible for long range planning and production issues for the company, while the Marketing Department Circle focuses on marketing with shorter time frames of individual marketing campaigns or functions. In Charles' Publicity Unit Circle the time frame is even shorter. Susan, as the operational leader, addresses the next newsletter and the next user conference when working with the members of the circle. When she and Charles participate in the Marketing Circle, however, their time horizon is at least three years and includes the consideration of new products and

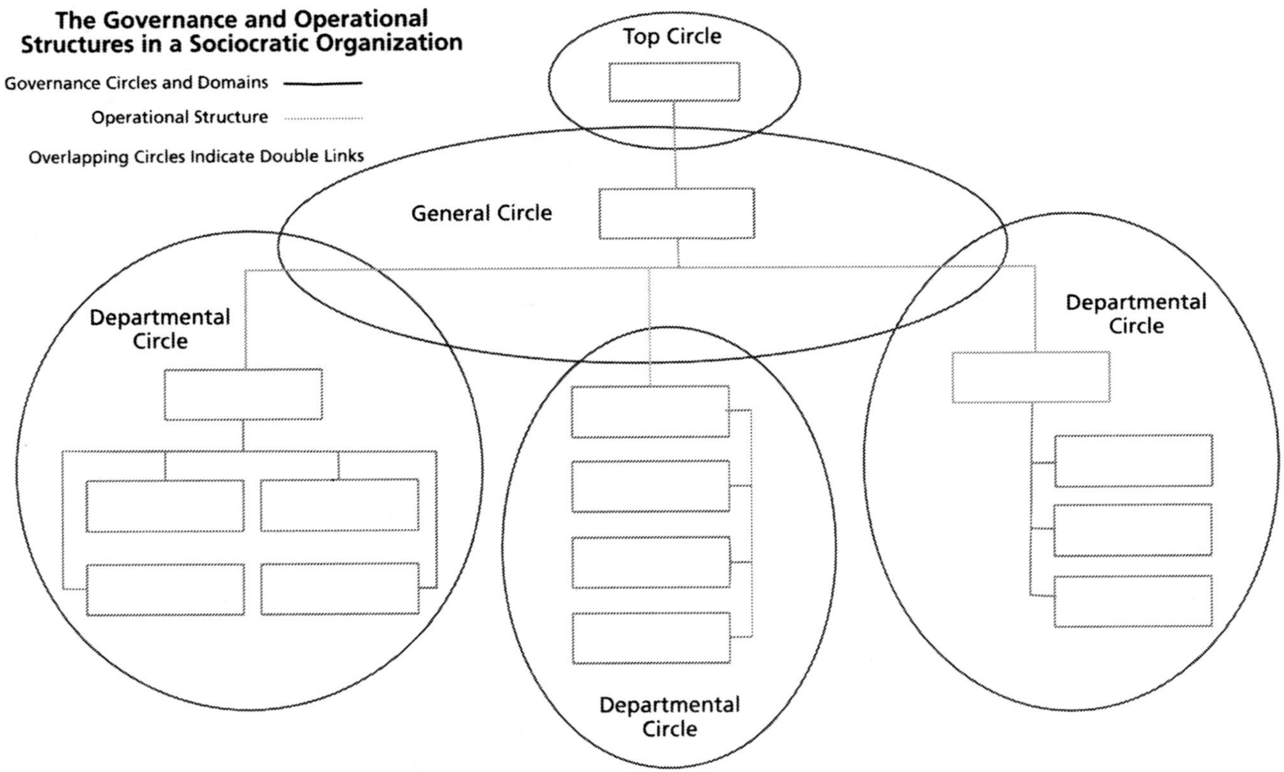

The Governance and Operational Structures in a Sociocratic Organization

Governance Circles and Domains ————
Operational Structure ⋯⋯⋯⋯⋯⋯
Overlapping Circles Indicate Double Links

Top Circle

General Circle

Departmental Circle

Departmental Circle

Departmental Circle

Figure 6.4 The Governance and Operational Structures in a Sociocratic Organization. The circle structure for governance encompasses the hierarchical structure for day-to-day operations in each domain or area of decision making.

multiyear budgets.

Figure 6.4 is a diagram of a simple sociocratic structure with the generic names for the circles: Top Circle, General Circle, and Department Circles. The number of levels and circles will differ from one organization to another depending on both the size and the level of complexity. Some organizations will have many circles but only three levels; others many circles and many levels. Circle names will also be determined by the organization. The generic names are useful, however, for understanding the various functions of circles in the hierarchy of work. The department circles will be of two kinds: (1) those responsible for fulfilling the aim of the organization and (2) those responsible for supporting the aim-fulfilling circles by providing the administrative functions of accounting, personnel, and facilities maintenance. The general circle brings both types of department circles together to determine overall operational policy.

Department circles include members who work together functionally. In a factory, for example, they might be particular sections of an assembly line. In a large high school, they might be one academic department. In a community organization they might be membership, programming, legislation, and events.

The general circle includes the operational department leaders, representatives selected by the department circles, and the general manager or CEO. The general circle selects the operational leaders of the departments and makes decisions that affect the general policies of the departments.

The top circle includes external experts, the general manager or CEO, and the chosen representative(s) from the general circle. The top circle selects the top executive officer (general manager, CEO) and focuses on long-range planning and relationships with external organizations.

The top circle's external experts serve as full members of the top circle and include a technical expert who is familiar with the aim of the organization, a social or organizational expert, a legal or governmental expert, and a financial or economic expert who can represent stockholders' interests or the interests of funding agencies or donors in the case of a non-profit organization. By including experts along with the CEO and elected representatives from the general circle, the top circle encompasses the interests of the organization itself, its members, its environment, and its profession or industry. By connecting the organization to its environment, the external members of the top circle prevent the organization from becoming a closed system. In doing so they help the organization guide itself dynamically.

A top circle always includes the CEO or equivalent and representatives selected by the general circle. In many organizations the traditional board, consisting only of outsiders, has an autocratic relationship with the CEO and all other employees. This relationship is not the case in sociocratic organizations where not only the CEO but other members of the general circle are elected to be members of the top circle. Within the top circle, consent decision-making and reframing relationships through double-linking allows the CEO, elected representatives, and external experts to work together as true partners in developing policy.

Other Circles

Another type of circle not yet mentioned is the helping circle. The aim of a helping circle is policy preparation. Helping circles are temporary circles created as the need arises, depending on problems regarding policy or execution, marketing tasks, research assignments, etc., and formed by people from existing circles and reinforced, if necessary, by invited external experts. For example, a helping circle composed of people from different parts of the organization might be set up to prepare a marketing strategy plan for a potential new client. This usage is typical in a highly matrixed organization.

It is also possible to form a sub-helping circle from a helping sub-circle in order to take on smaller tasks, pieces of the whole, for greater efficiency. Helping circles recommend but do not make policy, because establishing policy is the prerogative of the circle or circles that have brought the helping circle into being.

CHAPTER SEVEN

New Leadership Strategies

❧❧

When we hear *leader*, we often think of exceptional people—scientists who discover cures for deadly diseases and actors who inspire generations of audiences. Perhaps we think of those who demonstrate extraordinary courage in unusual circumstances like military leaders or astronauts, or charismatic, powerful people who make decisions, control money, and hire and fire other people at will. Thus, the modern CEO like Jack Welch has become a legend. Welch has ten best-selling books focusing on his leadership at General Electric including *Jack Welch on Leadership, Big Shots: Business the Jack Welch Way, Jack Welch and the 4 E's of Leadership, Jack Welch and the GE Way, The GE Way Fieldbook*, and *Winning.*

The sociocratic concept of leadership goes much deeper than the exceptional person. In the sociocratic organization, leadership is the responsibility of each person in the organization and is encouraged by both the governing principles and the organizational structure.

One of the difficulties in understanding leadership is that studies in leadership first assume that leadership is a unique personal quality and then often assume a difference in leadership between presidents and managers, between managers and first line supervisors, between transformational leadership and transactional leadership, and so on. From this viewpoint, leadership is one thing for the board of directors, another for a floor supervisor, and still another for a peace activist or meeting facilitator. This approach has led to definitions of leadership as lists of specific skills. One definition lists eleven skills and another four. These lists of skills lead to arguments about how the pie should be sliced but ignore the nature of the pie. In particular, they ignore the relationship between leadership and the nature of work.

Scholars conducting research on leadership observe and conduct case studies of the most successful leaders. Since they collect their data in organizations using autocratic command structures, a structure that severely limits the nature and quality of leadership that can occur within it, these studies reflect a very narrow definition of leadership. As we have seen in the example of Henry Ford and his assembly line, authoritarian structures constrict rather than encourage leadership.

Sociocratic organizations approach leadership very differently. First, they distinguish between leadership roles and leadership functions. When most of us think of leadership, we think of the leadership role—the president, the boss, the person who tells everyone else what to do. In sociocratic organizations, leaders are not autocrats. The responsibilities of operational leaders are assigned by consent, first by the circle that selects them for a leadership role, and then by the circle whose work they lead. The responsibilities of operational leaders are thus defined by everyone affected by them.

While these operational leadership roles are very important in sociocracy and each working unit has an identified leader, there is more to leadership than fulfilling a role. There are leadership functions, among them the ability to stimulate ourselves and others to action, to evaluate and plan, to obtain and allocate resources, to define tasks and determine the required results, to initiate ideas, and to share the risks and rewards of implementing them. These leadership functions are expected of everyone—each person is expected to think like a leader—to become a co-entrepreneur.

Leadership is expected of everyone in the circle as one part of the circular process, the leading-doing-measuring cycle that ensures quality. It encourages everyone to take on some piece of leadership—even if it is only to structure the way one leads oneself. Viewing leadership as just one part of the circular process frees the operational leader from many stereotypes developed in autocratic organizations. For example, an autocratic leader is encouraged to avoid expressing uncertainty. In sociocratic organizations, uncertainty is an important part of the process of seeking the best solution. A leader can be both strong and uncertain.

Electing Leaders

The principle of consent applies to the assignment of functions nd tasks and to the choice of leaders in a sociocratic organization.

The Fourth Governing Principle

Circles elect people to functions and tasks by consent after open discussion.

When it is time for department circles to elect people to functions and tasks, circle members define the associated responsibilities, qualifications, and term of service. Nominations are made and discussed openly with all members of the circle present. Discussion focuses on the job requirements and each nominee's ability to fulfill them. In many instances the choice may be clear after little discussion and the election leader may propose a choice. The process is complete when everyone consents. (See Chapter 11, "Electing People," for a more detailed description of this process.)

While foreign to most organizations, this process is a highly affirming one in which people are openly appreciated and acknowledged for their strengths in the context of the aims of the organization. It produces a strong working group because it ensures that those elected for a task know they have the full support of their colleagues and will understand what their colleagues expect of them. Ensuring that everyone accepts the final selection as the best choice reduces friction and increases productivity.

The sociocratic election process has none of the winner-loser celebrations that we see in majority voting, none of the mystery that surrounds a nominating committee process, and none of the jealousy, anger, puzzlement, or despair that can arise when the boss announces an unexplained choice. The result has a positive effect on the way everyone works together and ultimately circle development.

Leadership as a Function of Work

While sociocratic organizations extend both the rights and the responsibilities of leadership to all members of the organization this does not mean that they eliminate the hierarchy that is typical of authoritarian organizations—rather, they use it differently. A sociocratic hierarchy grows out of the work process, not the structure of who has power over whom. It is important to understand this distinction because many of us reject or misunderstand the importance of the hierarchy in organizations and thus reject sociocratic ideas as well. Arthur Koestler (1905-1983), a multi-disciplinary thinker who wrote extensively on science topics, addressed the problem of hierarchies that many of us feel:

> Unfortunately, the term "hierarchy" itself is rather unattractive and often provokes an emotional resistance. It is loaded with military and ecclesiastic associations, or evokes the "pecking hierarchy" of the barnyard, and thus conveys the impression of a rigid, authoritarian structure, whereas in the present theory a hierarchy consists of autonomous, self-governing holons endowed with varying degrees of flexibility and freedom. (Koestler 1980)

Koestler's "holon," and the resultant "holarchy," a word that Koestler coined that has been picked up by Ken Wilber (1996) and others, is analogous to the circle in the sociocratic organization. Circles, like holons, are semi-autonomous and self-organizing, and at the same time, hierarchically arranged and interdependent.

Understanding how the hierarchy of work relates to the hierarchical structure of circles can be seen in our example of producing a flower garden. To design a garden one must choose the colors and textures, and make budget decisions about plants vs. seeds, annuals vs. perennials, etc. Choosing the specific plants requires decisions about budget. Will they be annuals or perennials? Plants or seeds? Then finding the plants or seeds. Planning and purchasing is followed by actual planting. Planting requires coordination pf plants, seeds, and workers with the weather. The soil must be prepared before the actual planting. All these steps must occur in a certain order.

Then comes the process of watering, fertilizing, and pruning. Followed by preparation for the next season. Each of these steps must occur in a particular order and its success is determined by how well the step before it is accomplished. This is the hierarchy of work which forces its own hierarchy of action on the process of creating a garden.

Now imagine that this garden is the size of a football field—a park or a botanical garden. Each step in the process of designing and planting becomes a task involving many people, and probably several organizations. In addition, if there are many people involved, some of the tasks might take place simultaneously—if they are well coordinated. While one set of people is obtaining approval of the design by the city council, another set could be researching the cost of plants and seeds. Once the design is done, one group could be preparing the soil while another is procuring the plants. This requires careful planning so the plants are not ordered before the soil is ready or the budget approved.

This is why sociocratic organizations are built on a structure that, as Koestler says, is so "unattractive" to many people. The hierarchy structures communications concerning related tasks and controls complex tasks so they are executed efficiently.

Unlike autocratic organizations, sociocratic organizations include bottom-up controls that counter-balance and correct top-down controls. A sociocratic organization could just as well be represented by a bottom-archy as illustrated in Figure 7.1. In fact, a sociocratic organization is both a hierarchy and a bottom-archy.

By emphasizing top-down decision making, an autocratic hierarchy can easily damage itself because there are few mechanisms, like consent, to ensure accurate feedback. Leadership becomes associated with charisma and gaining power. Turf battles begin to take precedence over functional work relationships and productivity declines.

We see the limits of this phenomenon in research that looks closely at leaders in measurably outperforming companies. In *Good to Great*, Jim Collins discusses the factors that enabled the good companies, the already outstanding, to become great companies. While General Electric, lead by Jack Welch, outperformed the market by 2.8 times over the fifteen years from 1985 to 2000, when it was considered to be

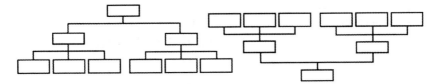

Figure 7.1 Hierarchy and Bottom-archy. A sociocratic organization is both a hierarchy and a bottom-archy of governing relationships between semi-autonomous, self-organizing circles. Communications and control, the power of organization, flows both up and down the organization.

the best managed corporation in America, the great companies, most with leaders you have never heard of, outperformed the general market by 6.9 times during the periods in which they tipped from good to great. Collins and his research associates discovered that the leaders of these great companies were more concerned with performance in their companies than with anything else.

> The good-to-great leaders never wanted to become larger-than-life heroes. They never aspired to be put on a pedestal or become unreachable icons. They were seemingly ordinary people quietly producing extra-ordinary results. (Collins 2001)

This exemplifies the kind of leadership that each person is expected to display in the sociocratic organization.

Strategic Planning & The Art of War

Sociocratic methods are both highly conceptual and fundamentally practical. They appeal to those who appreciate complex theoretical principles as well as those who appreciate direct and efficient action. Both require good strategic planning. But what is strategic planning? Fundamentally, it is a detailed policy.

Military theorists have written most of the works on strategic planning. The earliest in Western cultures was the prominent Prussian military theorist and educator Carl von Clausewitz who published a famous treatise on strategic planning in 1832, *On War*. It is still one of the most influential works on military strategy. In the first framework for formulating strategic plans, he distinguished between short-term tactics, which can change from day-to-day, and long-term strategies, which do not. The purpose of day-to-day operations is to execute the short-term tactical decisions that fulfill the long-term strategies.

Strategic planning, Clausewitz said, should include:

- a clear overall objective,
- rational estimations of resources that will be required and are currently available,
- contingency plans to account for practicalities,
- assurance of good sources of information, and
- identification of good leaders.

He emphasized that strategy includes planning for all foreseeable events and identifying sufficient resources to cope with the unforeseeable.

Here, we clearly see leadership as a function, not as a role. Although Clausewitz, who was familiar only with autocratic methods of organization, would have limited these functions to the person filling the leadership role, we can see that each person, at least in a non-military organization, must include such planning at the level of their own work and understand how their work fits into the planning of the larger organization if they are to function effectively.

In Clausewitz, there are also startling similarities to modern non-linearity and complexity theory, some of the same theories that Endenburg used in developing the principles for sociocratic organization. Clausewitz said building the strength of an organization was in developing its human capital, not in teaching people techniques as Henry Ford was later to do in designing his assembly line. Since the world changes moment-to-moment, knowing specific techniques is of little long-term value. People must understand the underlying principles so they can produce new technologies as they become necessary. Good information is key, but leadership skills are greater predictors of ultimate success.

In the 1970s, when the Japanese suddenly burst forth in world markets with superior and much cheaper technology, Sun Tzu's *The Art of War*, written in 500 BC, was cited as their inspiration. It quickly became required reading in management programs and students were all encouraged to become samurai. Sun Tzu praised subtlety and swift action with as little loss as possible. He advised against physical violence. "Why destroy," he asks, "when you can win by stealth and cunning? To subdue the enemy's forces without fighting is the summit of skill." He counsels that the effective general undermines the enemies' alliances, morale, and economic foundations. Physical force is not the best weapon, Sun Tzu said, nor destruction the best value. Organization and leadership require more skill and cunning.

Deficiencies of the War Analogy

While both Clausewitz and Sun Tzu were excellent theorists, the use of war analogies in defining good leadership and strategic planning requires viewing success as a struggle to defeat an enemy. The object of leadership becomes conquest rather than accomplishment. Even though the focus of war in Sun Tzu's terms is more subtle, to acquire without destroying, the emphasis is still on victory over others.

Military leaders, particularly those who are successful wartime leaders, are not necessarily successful leaders in other kinds of organizations. For example, Ulysses S. Grant was a business failure both before the Civil War and after his presidency. Yet he was by far the North's best military strategic thinker, bringing the ferocious and brilliant tactician Robert E. Lee to submission. Military organizations are highly structured with clearly defined aims and often a captive workforce. Their world-view is black and white; they polarize in order to focus energies and to emphasize the importance of the battle. War is literally life or death and very immediate.

If war leaders are to be emulated, then an enemy has to be identified. More often than not, the only enemy in sight is the competition. Leaders focus on destroying the competition rather than on serving the best interests of the consumer or the client. The American Federation of Teachers (AFT) and the National Education Association (NEA) for example, battle against each other for the right to represent teachers. Rather than a strategic plan that works for the interests of teachers, they spend great sums of money defeating each other in elections. As a strategy, this places the emphasis on the competitor, not the client—the still under-paid and under-respected teacher, or the under-served students.

The Strategic Planning Process

Sociocratic organizations seek leaders who understand both aim and strategy. Selecting leaders is done in the context of a new strategic plan that in a sociocratic organization is done at least every two years. It begins with the top circle, moves to the general circle, and then moves to each of the department circles. The process begins with an examination of the organization's aim. "Are we providing exactly what our clients now want?" The general circle examines the aim in respect to long-range planning and abstract goals. As the process moves down the hierarchy, the strategy becomes more concrete and more focused on tasks related to day-to-day operations. Each circle adjusts its aim to align with the new overall aim.

Just as important, planning moves back up the organization again as each circle and each person reviews the plan and suggests corrections and additions. The plan may look very good at an abstract level but not be possible for some units to implement. Changes may need to be made in the more abstract goals so the more tangible goals can be met.

The strategic plan in a sociocratic organization is subject to consent just like other policy decisions. Based on the comments of the circles above and below, each circle in turn adjusts its written strategy and reformulates its work process. After the adjustments in the circles are completed, each person revises their own strategy, including what they would like to achieve in their own job, how to accomplish that, and how to allocate their own time and resources. Then a round of elections begins. Each circle elects or reaffirms current operational leaders. The circles reassign their members to new tasks that reflect the new aims. And they reaffirm or elect new representatives.

Everyone records the decisions made during this process in their personal logbooks. These logbooks contain all the organization's working documents. In a sociocratic organization, everyone has direct access to all policy documents and any other records relating to their work. This transparency is essential if each person is to be expected to assume the responsibility of leadership and participate equivalently in decision-making.

The double-linked circle structure carries the strategic planning process and leadership expectations deeply into the organization, linking long-term strategic planning directly to short-term tactical planning and to day-to-day operations. Leadership and strategy are thus deeply integrated into the work process at all levels of the sociocratic organization.

CHAPTER EIGHT

Fair Compensation & Free Organizations

The question of what is fair compensation is closely related to the rights and powers of corporations and other organizations. The rights of corporations to champion their own interests have evolved throughout history. When the United States gained freedom from the British, it also gained freedom from English law. The fledgling states granted corporations charters for a limited number of years for limited purposes. The states could withdraw these charters at any time if the corporations exceeded these limited purposes, and states did not necessarily renew them. Only "we the people," the local government, could decide whether to renew corporate charters. Thus, a community could decide whether a corporation was in the best interests of the community. This all changed in 1886.

The most influential decision that gave corporations the vast power they have today came when "personhood" was legally awarded to corporations, giving them the same rights as individual citizens. This personhood decision may have been an error made by a Supreme Court clerk in the case of *Santa Clara County v. Southern Pacific Railroad*, but it became a legal precedent and stands today.

As "persons," corporations can use the Fourteenth Amendment to protect themselves against infringement of their right to do business as they determine appropriate. The Fourteenth Amendment says:

> All persons born or naturalized in the United States and subject
> to the jurisdiction thereof, are citizens of the United States and of

the State wherein they reside. No State shall make or enforce any law which shall abridge the privileges or immunities of citizens of the United States; nor shall any State deprive any person of life, liberty, or property, without due process of law; nor deny to any person within its jurisdiction the equal protection of the laws.

Ironically, the court did not address the Thirteenth Amendment that states:

Neither slavery nor involuntary servitude, except as a punishment for crime whereof the party shall have been duly convicted, shall exist within the United States, or any place subject to their jurisdiction.

Thus, today, corporations are "legal persons" that can be owned as legal slaves.

The court's application of the Fourteenth Amendment gives corporations enormous power to conduct business with minimal government intervention or oversight. In 1790, about 90% of adults in the United States worked in independent farming families. Today, corporations, both profit and non-profit, structure the social and economic circumstances under which we work and live. In addition, because neither individuals nor local governments have the resources to conduct civil litigation equal to those of corporations, corporations have extensive control, for good or evil, over our lives. Recent lawsuits against cigarette companies are the rare exception.

As discussed earlier, corporations have also provided us with most, if not all, of the modern comforts we enjoy. An end to corporations would end many ills but would also end many comforts. What sociocracy promises are more effective, inclusive, and responsive organizations, including corporations. While corporations have been publicized recently as the most egregiously unethical of our organizations, similar problems are present in governments and associations, where sociocracy can help as well. To understand how, we must first look at the concepts of profit and compensation.

Profit as Measurement

Like *competition*, the word *profit* has assumed negative connotations for some and an obsession for others. It has become so emotionally charged that one of its main properties is under-appreciated. This property is its ability to convey information.

Organizational development consultants find that the number one problem that concerns all clients is "lack of communication." Lack of communication, or information sharing, dominates the work of organizational development consultants to such a degree that many see it as a superficial description of what must be deeper dysfunctions. (Wheatley, 1992) How can communications cause problems in so many varied organizations?

The fact is that moving information from one person to the next, much less from one department to another or one division of a multinational corporation to another, is very difficult. It requires finding a way to reduce misinterpretation or distortion. This is very hard. The most accurate form of information is numbers. If a piece of information can be described as a number, it is least likely to be misinterpreted.

In the circular process of leading-doing-measuring, profit is a measurement that gives feedback. It conveys information. As we have seen, feedback in the form of measurement is necessary for steering. The accuracy, appropriateness, and timeliness of feedback determines the ability of the leading function to evaluate and direct effectively. Monetary profit, properly reported, is a highly accurate and easily communicated measurement.

Monetary profit information can give insight into:

- How well individuals are able to perform
- Whether competitors are achieving better results
- Whether compensation adequately recognizes achievement
- The degree to which the organization is sustainable.

Profit, however, is not just about money. Profit includes all measures of success. When money is the only measure used, the information can be misleading.

In an organization devoted to the elimination of land mines, for example, money may be one measure since money may be needed to support communications, staff, and volunteer coordination. But the organization would also need to pay attention to other measurements of profit like the number of governments that are allowing inspectors into their countries, the number of mine fields cleared, the number of new mine fields discovered, the number of countries who have agreed not to use land mines, etc. An organization like this might show a very high monetary profit in terms of donations and grants from foundations, but if the other measures do not show growth, the organization would soon fail. It would not be fulfilling its mission and would eventually go bankrupt, socially as well as financially. Funds would be withdrawn and it would not be sustainable.

Profit is the total result of all activities within the enterprise. If a non-profit organization is profitable in the broad sense of benefiting from exchange, then donors will keep donating, legislatures will keep funding, and volunteers will keep volunteering. This non-monetary measurement of profit is difficult because it is more difficult to quantify, but to create and manage a dynamic organization, measuring it is essential.

Non-monetary measurements can also be more difficult to define and if improperly defined can make an organization dysfunctional. For example, Deming found that one of his clients, the Veteran's Administration (VA) hospitals, was measuring success in terms of "patient bed days" delivered. The hospitals had a terrible reputation and hospital stays were much longer than in other hospitals. Because of the measurement that defined success, the hospitals were loath to release a patient until another patient was available to fill the bed. Deming convinced the VA to change the measure of success to the number of "patients made healthy." "Healthy" was then defined as a patient who did not return to the hospital for at least 30 days after discharge. As a result, the whole behavior of the staff changed and the reputation of the hospitals improved.

On the other hand, an organization that measures itself only with monetary data from business operations such as buying, selling, market position, production method, etc., is not fully measuring its exchange with society. True, a business makes a monetary exchange in the form of taxes, but it also makes a number of non-monetary exchanges that ultimately affect its overall profitability. These include effects on environmental resources and the social aspects of effects on employees and nearby neighborhoods. Some accountants may attempt to place a monetary value on these factors, calling them "goodwill" but in most respects there is no attempt to measure fully the social impact of an organization on a community, certainly not the negative ones.

The failure to measure non-monetary profits (and losses) is as short-sighted and ultimately self-defeating for corporations as it is for non-profit organizations to fail to measure their monetary profits (and losses).

Exchange Processes

An aim is a product or service, differentiated from other aims, and defined from the point of view of the client. An aim establishes the basis for an exchange by creating an overlap connecting supply and demand, the company and the client. In our complex society, we all have more needs than we can fill by our own means. We must enter into an exchange with others in our environment to fulfill all our needs. To do this, we must produce something to exchange.

A good exchange is one that is beneficial to all participants. For example, if I make only shoes and you make only shirts, I lack shirts and you lack shoes. If we exchange some of your shirts for some of my shoes, we have both profited because we are both better off than we were before the exchange.

"Non-profit organizations" are misnamed because they would not exist unless they obtained more money than they spent. They would have no savings to cover losses, no reserves to replace equipment, and no ability to grow and change with the environment. It is more accurate to say that they are "indirect client organizations" because their income comes from a different source than the one they serve. A direct client business like a bakery sells bread directly to a customer. The source of "profit" is the same as the person served.

While many organizations often receive support directly from clients, non-profit organizations receive their support from governments, foundations, and donors who determine the value of services rather than the clients who in this instance may not pay for the services or have control over the exchange.

Producing more goods or services than the organization needs is the only way it can continue to meet all its needs. Without a profit, no organization is sustainable. The aim defines the basis of this exchange. In this respect, there is no difference between profit and non-profit organizations. Each type of organization should be measuring its exchanges and its profit from those exchanges. Without this information, good steering is impossible.

Self-Optimization

Why do we work? Is it our desire to satisfy our physical needs or perhaps a fear of scarcity? Based on the work of John Forbes Nash, who in 1994 along with two other game theorists won the Nobel Prize in Economics and whose life was the subject of the film, *A Beautiful Mind*, sociocracy assumes there is basic "economic motive" in the fact of our being alive. The consequence is a natural drive toward improvement or "optimization" of our resources—again, not necessarily using money as a goal. The drive to optimize might center on one's skill in body painting, the number of people one can make laugh, or the number of songs sung. This assumption about optimization as a basic economic motive has far-reaching consequences.

All exchange processes are self-optimizing regardless of whether they are purposely constructed or naturally occurring. If they cease to be self-optimizing, it is because their aim is gone and they cease to be dynamic. If they cease to be dynamic, they become rigid and die. Self-optimization results from the continual measuring activity that occurs in a properly constructed circular process, one that includes leading-doing-measuring. In any dynamic process there is a continuous and active search for a better way of reaching an aim. A shortage of resources required for production, for example, need not result in a mindset of scarcity and an unthinking reduction in productivity.

Scarcity is a passive linear concept. It assumes limited resources and a fixed ability to acquire. It can also be used by those with power as a trick to maintain power-over: "If you don't do as I say, you'll lose your job." Scarcity thinking does not recognize the dynamic possibilities of exchange processes to create value. Unemployment can exist in an economy where there is plenty of work to do. Because scarcity as a motivation for work is a linear concept, sociocracy views the problem of poor economy as a lack of organization. This thought is essentially the one John Stuart Mill expressed when he observed that society's problems of scarcity were not due to lack of wealth but were caused by inadequate distribution of resources.

Transparency

Because all levels of the sociocratic organization are involved in decision-making, access to the information used for measurement is vital to everyone in the organization. Therefore sociocratic financial reporting systems show both the profit of the company as a whole and the team and individual contributions to that profit. Over time, the fear that data will be manipulated and used against workers diminishes for several reasons: the safety guaranteed by consent decision-making, the guaranteed base wage, and the transparency of operations in a sociocratic organization.

In an autocratically structured company, only the owners or shareholders and sometimes the top management (in the form of bonuses) "experience the measurement" of profits. In a sociocratically structured organization, all participants share in profits or losses.

The Sociocratic Compensation Structure

As we discussed earlier, in addition to money, profit may be reported in any terms that are relevant to the organization: the number of refugees resettled, reading levels increased, consumer complaints reduced, monetary surplus, etc. For purposes of the following discussion about the distribution of profit, however, we will focus on money since that is the most easily exchanged form of profit.

In most organizations, there are two kinds of participants:

- Day-to-day, labor-providing participants
- Shareholders, or for non-profits, donors or sponsors

Both categories are equally important to the existence and to the success of the organization. In sociocratic organizations, both labor and shareholders are guaranteed compensation in the form of a Guaranteed Base Wage (GBW). For labor, this guaranteed payment is based on the market value of each person's functions and tasks and on the ability of the organization to sustain these payments. The GBW is not related to profit distribution. In the literal Dutch translation, it is an "existence possibility guarantee." The equivalent for investors or donors, their GBW, is a guaranteed basic return on investment. For donors or sponsors, this guaranteed basic return might be delivery of services to target populations.

In addition to the GBW, each participant in the organization, whether wage earner or investor, receives variable or "measuring" payments that bring the circular process of leading-doing-measuring into the wage/share structure. The specific structure of measurement payments, which are based on the wage/share ratios, are recorded in the bylaws of the organization. Everyone has access to reports on the organization's profits and losses and the variable payments made.

If variable payments are made too infrequently, participants might not get enough feedback. Annual payments in December might not give good information about efforts made early in February, nor distinguish between the efforts made in February and those made in August. Measurements need to be received in a more direct and timely manner to be reliably used for accurate measurement. Therefore, sociocracy uses a two-part incentive system: a Long-Term Measurement (LTM) and a Short-Term Measurement (STM).

Depending on the industry or services provided, the STM may cover the duration of a single project or, in the case of a long-term project, a period measured by a particular milestone. The amount paid is the difference between the originally estimated profits and the actual result. If the result is lower than projected, there is no STM payment, and furthermore, the shortfall must be recovered before more STM payments, or LTM payments, can be made. (See Chapter 13, "Money as Measurement," for more information.)

This variable payment system is not the same as piecework where people are paid for each piece of work completed. They are different in two ways. Firstly, the GBW is paid without reference to the STM and LTM payments, and secondly this compensation system applies, without exception, to everyone, from shareholders to board members to mail room employees. It is a steering device only.

Because the compensation structure ensures that all participants in a sociocratic organization share in profits or losses, they share a deep common interest. Everyone benefits, or suffers when profit falls. This also means that their responsibilities are more consciously experienced in relation to each other, and the distrust and competition between employer and employee, senior or junior, no longer has a reason to exist. Everyone in the same boat.

Investment Capital

But if everyone shares in the profits of the organization, how do businesses attract investors? How do they finance start up and expansion?

In principle, the various choices for attracting investors who will provide capital for growth and development remain the same in a sociocratic organization as in a traditional autocratic organization. A sociocratic organization can attract the capital it needs in the traditional way: loans, credit, mortgages, bonds, shares, and all other possibilities. Providers of capital participate through their representatives in the Top Circle.

In autocratic organizations, for profit or not for profit, the board of directors constitutes the governing body and sets organizational policy. The shareholders, sponsors, or donors influence policy through the board of directors, but neither the staff nor other members of the organization set policy unless they have personal influence over members of the board, which is not common.

In a sociocratic organization, all members of the organization participate in setting policy. The Top Circle includes the functions of the traditional board of directors, like long range planning, but the Top Circle includes representatives from other parts of the organization and its decisions are subject to consent. In addition, because the organization's plans and finances are transparent, available for review by all members of the organization, the activities of the Top Circle

Figure 8.1 Our Boat. In a sociocratic organization, everyone is in the same boat in terms of compensation based on profits and losses.

are open to the organization in a way that most board decisions and actions are not. Later, we will discuss ways to maintain transparency within the company without leaking key information to competitors.

Another distinction between an autocratically structured and a sociocratically structured company is that in an autocratically structured company, the shareholders determine *in retrospect* how the profit is going to be shared. It may be distributed to shareholders as dividends, reinvested in one or another aspects of the organization, paid to the CEO as a bonus, put in reserves, etc. In a sociocratic organization, the circle structure establishes the distribution of profits (or losses) *in advance* so that everyone knows what to expect and the distributions are more likely to be made on the basis of solid planning rather than on the whims or political pressure exerted by one group.

A sociocratic organization is not an employee-owned company. Most employee-owned companies are autocratically structured. All or most of the employees are shareholders and share profits as shareholders but they do not share in policy making. A board of directors will make decisions just as they do in non-employee owned companies. As employees they will not participate in policy decisions, make the day-to-day operational decisions, determine the best way to complete their assigned tasks, or participate in an incentive plan. The source of their control is still ownership. As employees, they are not enfranchised; they have no voice in how the company is run except

RIGHTS AND REWARDS OF STAKEHOLDERS COMPARED

	Fixed Compensation	Variable Compensation	Policy Decision-Making
In Autocratic Corporations:			
Capital Providing	–	x	x
Labor Providing	x	–	–
In Sociocratic Corporations:			
Capital Providing	x	x	x
Labor Providing	x	x	x

Figure 8.2 **Rights and Rewards of Stakeholders Compared.** The rights of stakeholders in an autocratic corporation vary according to whether a stakeholder is providing capital or labor. In a sociocratic organization, all stakeholders have equivalent access to both compensation and governance decisions.

indirectly, as owners, by voting for members of the board.

Further, because control of an employee-owned company rests with a majority of the shares, employee-owned companies are limited in their ability to raise outside capital. Sociocratic corporations, however, can freely raise capital through the sale of stock without losing control of the organization. A sociocratic organization is controlled by all the participants—shareholders, labor, management, volunteers, etc.—through their participation in the double-linked network of circles. Figure 8.2 summarizes this discussion of compensation structure and investment capital.

No Owners, No Slaves

Traditionally those who provide the capital own the organization and control it by virtue of that ownership. Capital may come from shareholders, a foundation that provides funding, or an individual owner. The employees as shareholders may own it. But whoever provides the funds owns the company and can sell, close, or trade it. In other words, they can do whatever they wish with the organization. Owners view the company as an object like a car or a machine or an animal, like a horse, even though people are involved. As discussed earlier, according to the *Santa Clara County v. Southern Pacific Railroad* decision by the United States government in 1886, corporations have the rights of personhood. They have the right to exist in the same way a person has a right to exist. But, unlike free persons, the company, along with its employees, can be owned and traded like slaves.

A sociocratic corporation, however, owns itself, like any free citizen. The corporation is not a possession. It arises from the people who create and recreate it each day. The participants in the organization can agree to form alliances or to merge with other organizations but the organization cannot be "taken over" or sold against its will. The participants as a group, including the shareholders, are the organization and no part can sell them or the organization without the consent of the other parts. As a free corporation, no longer an object, a sociocratic organization is liberated to operate like a fully living organism. As with a person, emancipation has a strong beneficial impact on its vitality and profitability.

PART III

How It Works

Organizing Our Strengths

☙❦❧

In 1876, in response to his observations of great disorder in debate in democratic organizations around the country, General Henry M. Robert, an expert on parliamentary procedure, wrote *A Pocket Manual of Rules of Order for Deliberative Assemblies*. Now known as *Robert's Rules of Order*, it has become the standard reference for applying parliamentary procedure in the United States. Robert's aim was to ensure fair debate, but his work was based on the assumption that majority rule was the best decision-making method possible. Compared to autocratic decision-making, perhaps it was, but with sociocratic governance there is an even better method available. In this section of the text, "How It Works," we will explain what are essentially the "rules of order" of sociocratic organizations.

But before we go too far with that analogy, we must say that Gerard Endenburg didn't set out to create "his" rules of order nor are they rules in the same sense as those in Robert's rules. Sociocratic processes are based on scientific principles and are not Endenburg's personal invention. The four governing principles take what is known to be true in the physical and natural sciences and apply it by analogy to the governance and management of organizations. Robert's rules establish a logical order of debate (for example, points of information should be addressed before debate continues), but they are limited to debate and the functions of officers in regulating and recording debate. They have nothing to say about the organization of work or production. They do not address leadership, measurement, feedback, or any other functions necessary to for organizations to govern themselves.

Robert's rules are valuable in large bodies where they bring discipline to debate and voting, but they can be overwhelming as well. The process of following them can divert attention from the basic argument. In parliamentary law, the only test of a good decision is the following of proper order of debate and the proper recording of the vote. Majority vote is the only judge of quality.

Sociocratic debate focuses on the argument, not the majority opinion. In sociocratic organizations, the argument is stated in the context of the aim. What is our aim? How can we best achieve it? Can everyone work toward the aim if we accept this proposal? To ensure that all members of the organization understand the aim of the organization, the aim of their department, and the aim of their own role in that organization, all functions and tasks are defined in terms of the aim. This focus is what makes sociocratic organizations more satisfying for their members and more powerful in doing their work.

Implementation

Installation of a sociocratic governance structure is led by an implementation circle. Using the circular process of leading-doing-measuring, the circle makes a plan, tries a small step, measures the results, then evaluates and adjusts the plan, repeating as necessary.

While some changes in production, services, or activities may occur, these are normally improvements that the sociocratic method reveals to be advisable, rather than changes required to accommodate the new governance system. For example, in a Dutch police organization the implementation circle decided to drastically reduce the number of reporting levels in its organization. In the United States, in a rapidly growing nonprofit organization with many local chapters and a very flat operational structure, implementation led to the creation of a regional structure, establishing a step in the hierarchy that did not previously exist. In other cases, the circle structure simply reflects the existing operational structure. Once in place, the circle structure guides the development of the operational structure.

How To

Part III, "How It Works" further explains sociocratic concepts as it explains how to apply them. We encourage you to read this section even if you do not have immediate plans to implement any of the methods. If you are already a member of a sociocratically governed organization, Part III can serve as a reference, providing a quick way to look up definitions and processes.

As with all such "how to" sections, this information is not a substitute for the advice of a professional sociocratic consultant who can address specific situations, but it is a good foundation for understanding which professional you may need and what the professional may be advising. (See Appendix D, "Sociocratic Centers & Consultants," to find a certified consultant.)

Sociocratic methods will continue to develop just as the scientific understandings from which they are derived develop. In this sense, the sociocratic method is a "tool," not a philosophy. Its only agenda, political theory, or moral stance is to establish and protect the equivalence of each person and enhance their ability to pursue happiness and prosperity. Equivalence and the power of the argument are the foundations of sociocratic governance.

Chapter Nine, "Circles & Implementation," outlines the process for beginning to structure your organization sociocratically. Chapter Ten, "Consent & Rounds," outlines the process of conducting circle meetings and explains how making space for each person in a circle meeting to speak maintains equivalence and ensures that each person can register objections when necessary. Chapter Eleven, "Electing People," discusses in detail how to elect people in open discussion by consent. Chapter Twelve, "Organizing Work," outlines the process of defining an aim and organizing the work process. Chapter Thirteen, "Money as Measurement," explains how the short and long term incentive payments are calculated.

These methods are simple but their careful application is important. In our experience, it is helpful to implement when connected with others who are implementing. The "Afterword" explains how to network with people who are learning and implementing sociocracy in their businesses and organizations.

CHAPTER NINE

Circles & Implementation

The first step in establishing a sociocratic governance structure in an organization is to form an implementation circle. The implementation circle members are typically a cross-section of the organization, including the top managers or officers in the current structure, representatives from the major departments or units, and staff members. The implementation circle receives training in sociocratic principles and methods and then determines the best ways to begin forming the double-linked circles that will become the new governance structure. It is important for the implementation circle to work with a certified sociocratic organizational consultant and for the whole circle to receive training.

The implementation circle functions sociocratically, applying the principle of consent, thus gaining important experience that can be later shared with the rest of the organization. The implementation circle's first steps, and those of each circle as it forms, are electing circle members to functions and tasks, establishing logbooks, planning its work process, and creating the circular process of leading-doing-measuring to guide the work of the circle.

The implementation circle also initiates the infrastructure for maintaining the governance system: the logbook systems for record keeping, policies for distributing minutes, regular meeting times, training current members of the organization, and orientation and training of new people who join the organization. As each circle is activated, it then assumes responsibility for its own process, including electing people to functions and tasks, implementing the leading-doing-measuring process for each area of its responsibility, and planning for the development of its members.

The implementation circle should plan the order of activation of the circles. If the top circle (including board of directors) has not been activated, it should be activated as soon as feasible. Sometimes the top circle is activated before the implementation circle, meaning it has already begun to operate sociocratically and has elected the implementation circle. In other cases the implementation circle begins functioning first. This order depends on the size,, complexity, and preferences of the organization.

Once the general circle and the top circle are established and fully functioning, the implementation circle dissolves, although some former members of the implementation circle may continue as internal trainers for the organization.

The top circle oversees completion of implementation and plans regular assessments of the sociocratic circle structure. Eventually the top circle amends the legal structure of the organization to establish consent as the basis of decision making, the circle as the context for governance decisions, double-linking between circles, and the election of persons to functions and tasks. Appendix E, "Operating Agreement and Bylaws for a Sociocratic Organization," is an example of how these clauses might be worded.

Circle Officers

There are four officers in each circle, each one elected by consent for a specific term:

1. Operational Leader
2. Circle Meeting Facilitator
3. Secretary and Logbook Keeper
4. Representative(s)

The next higher circle elects the operational leader of a department or team circle to supervise day-to-day operations. The higher circle also defines the circle's aim and domain of responsibility, and sets its budget. Typically, within the policies set by the circle and by higher circles, the operational leader has autocratic authority over daily operational decisions and task assignments. He or she may call staff meetings as needed and normally conducts the business of those meetings in the traditional autocratic manner. The circle may elect the operational leader to serve as the circle meeting facilitator or secretary and logbook keeper but *not* to serve as a representative.

The circle meeting facilitator is responsible for leading circle meetings and is elected by the circle. The facilitator should be someone who is adept at steering discussions, moving decisions forward, and keeping everyone focused on the aim of the meeting and the aim of the circle.

The circle also elects a person to serve as secretary and logbook keeper. The secretary is responsible for receiving agenda items, collaborating with the facilitator to prepare the agenda, sending out the agenda and meeting reminders, confirming attendance of key people or invited guests, preparing the meeting room, taking minutes of the meeting, and distributing minutes and other documents.

As logbook keeper the person is responsible for keeping the circle's logbooks up-to-date. The logbook will typically include a statement of the organization's vision, mission, and aim; bylaws; strategic plan; a diagram of the circle organization; organization and circle rules and procedures; meeting records; names and functions of circle members; and flow charts summarizing the leading, doing, and measuring activities of the circle. In addition, the logbook should include the circle's development plan.

The roles of the secretary and the logbook keeper may be filled by two persons based on the size of the circle and the complexity of the circle's work.

In addition to electing the circle meeting facilitator and secretary/logbook keeper, the circle elects one or more representatives to participate in the next higher circle. The representative may be the same person elected to be circle facilitator or secretary but may not be the person serving as the operational leader. As discussed in Chapter Six, "Steering & Structure," the representative carries information and power "up" the organization while the operational leader carries it "down." Like electricity, power can only go in one direction in one channel at one time. Double-linking ensures that the circular process elements of leading and measuring are preserved between circles.

The representative is not a mere vote carrier but one who participates fully, with consent, in both circles, using his or her best judgment
in making decisions, rather than functioning at the direction of an
electorate as delegates do. A representative must be able to understand and communicate the lower circle's interests and also be able to
participate in decisions at the higher level of abstraction.

A circle may have more than one representative based on the
complexity and needs of the circle. It may also elect additional
representative(s) to temporarily represent the circle in a specific
decision as in the case of the story of the worker who was elected to
participate in the top circle in order to present his idea for reassign-
ing the shipyard workers as salespeople to solicit new business rather
than being laid off. (For the full discussion, see Chapter Three, "The
History of Sociocratic Governance.")

Circle Meetings

Circle meetings are usually busy, even exciting events since they
make or delegate all the policy decisions that guide the day-to-day
operations of the circle. They are also forums to share the ideas and
knowledge of all members of the circle. The topics a circle might
address in any given meeting include:

- Vision, mission, and aim
- Policy and strategy plans
- Progress of the circle toward its aim
- Design of work processes
- Circle's organizational or operational design and procedures that
  flow from it
- Function and task descriptions of circle members
- Allocation of tasks and functions
- Addition or removal of someone from the circle
- The circle's development process (plans for training, teaching,
  and researching)

As discussed in Chapter Five, "Developing Quality," a circle is a group
of people with a common aim who make decisions together within
an agreed upon framework. It is semi-autonomous and self-organiz-

ing. It determines its own policies and decides how it will complete its work within the limits of its aim and budget. Thus, the structure of circle meetings differs from that of operational staff meetings. In a circle meeting, all members participate as peers and the subjects discussed focus on policy determination and planning. Sociocratic organizations continue to need periodic staff meetings to guide day-to-day operations, but they typically are needed less often because the work process designed by the circle encourages clearer delegation and more effective follow-up. In Chapter Thirteen, "Organizing Work," we will present a detailed discussion of the process of "producing organization."

As described above, the secretary is responsible for meeting logistics. Several days before the meeting, the secretary confers with the facilitator and the operational leader and publishes the agenda and supporting documents to all circle members.

A circle meeting follows a predictable pattern of four parts:

1. Opening Round
2. Administration
   (Announcements, Housekeeping, Agenda Setting, etc.)
3. Content (Agenda Items)
4. Closing Round

Holding the opening round before any other activity establishes the tone of the meeting as "we the people," allowing everyone to attune to each other and to the aim of the circle meeting.

Administrative details follow the opening round. They include any information that needs to be communicated and for which no discussion or decisions are required. Introduce guests, if necessary. Make announcements. Address logistics (Is the temperature of the room okay? Does anyone need a copy of the handout? etc.) Solicit objections to the minutes of the previous meeting and then adjust minutes, if necessary. The administrative details should end with consent to the agenda for the content part of the meeting. This agenda is the contract that members are making for the work of the meeting.

The content section usually has three kinds of agenda items: informational reports, policy proposals, and discussion of issues that may lead to proposals. If an agenda item is simply an informational report, such as a financial report, the policy decision is whether to accept the report. If it is a policy proposal, the decision will be whether to accept the proposal and/or who to elect for a function or task. Sometimes issues are discussed and proposals are developed in the meeting. All decisions are subject to the consent of all circle members. Consenting to proposals will be discussed more fully in Chapter Ten, "Consent & Rounds," which explains simple consent, consent with a proposal, and consent when developing a proposal.

A circle meeting will normally conduct its business in a combination of rounds, discussion, and dialogue. Rounds are very important in sociocracy because they establish equivalence between members and give each person not only an opportunity but an invitation to express objections. Chapter Ten, "Consent & Rounds," contains a detailed discussion of doing rounds.

The closing round is the "measuring" part of the meeting. Comments might address the questions: Did the meeting go well? What could have been improved? What was the quality of the discussion? Was the agenda completed? Are there any items that need to be revisited in the next meeting? How well was time managed? How are the members feeling?

Circle Meeting Minutes and the Logbook

Each circle, like a self-organizing living organism, is responsible for its own memory system, namely the logbook that contains minutes of meetings, policy decisions, strategic plans, work process documents, etc. Minutes of meetings should include:

1. Name of the Circle

2. Date and Time of the Meeting

3. Attendees

4. Text of Decisions

5. Closing Round Comments

It is usually not necessary to record verbatim comments. Taking detailed notes prevents the secretary from participating in the meeting and can lead to spending more time on the details of the minutes than is productive. On complex and difficult decisions, one or more members may request inclusion of a summary of the reasoning or assumptions made in reaching the decision so the rationale for the decision is clear, for example, when the circle's records are audited by an outside government or accrediting agency. If the circle holds an information gathering discussion, doing "picture forming," and consents to the resulting list of opportunities and issues, this list of items may be included in the minutes along with delegating the task of writing the proposal. Otherwise, only a record of decisions is required, including a record of the assignment of functions and tasks that may include a list of action items. Recording action items from the closing round such as "the room was too hot" or "we needed the documents earlier" may also be helpful reminders.

The circle should develop its own process of ensuring that circle members have prompt access to the minutes and a chance to express any paramount objections.

Additional Resources:

Appendix F, "Guide for Circle Meetings"
Appendix G, "Guide to the Implementation Process"
Appendix H, "Guide for Logbooks"

CHAPTER TEN

Consent & Rounds

There are many well-known skills and techniques for facilitating successful meetings, from flip chart skills to making eye-contact, and for secretaries, taking notes and keeping records. Many of these are useful for circle meetings and we have not repeated them here. We will only discuss the particular rhythm of the sociocratic circle meeting, and the use of rounds to maintain equivalence and make consent decisions.

Rounds

Facilitators use rounds in circle meetings for many purposes, but their essential function is to create and maintain equivalence. The more common are opening and closing rounds, reaction rounds, and consent rounds.

In a round, each person in the meeting is given an opportunity to speak in turn. The facilitator should begin the round by asking one person to speak first and each person will continue (or pass) moving clockwise or counter clockwise around the circle. The facilitator should sometimes choose a person across the circle and sometimes a few people to the right or left. This allows the facilitator to speak in the middle of the sequence instead of last and a different person to start each round. If the circle members are not sitting in a circle or around a conference table and there is confusion over who should speak next, the facilitator can indicate with a nod who should speak next. If the circle meeting is conducted by telephone or by video conferencing, it is helpful if the facilitator assigns circle positions to the participants using a virtual table or clock, "George is at 1:00, Marsha is at 2:00, etc."

It is a mistake to ask, "Who would like to start?" for two reasons. First, the facilitator should *lead* and the circle will be more comfortable with clear direction. Second, what if the person who volunteers to start is in a horrible mood and negatively impacts the tone of the meeting? Or if several people want to start? Choosing between them immediately affects one key purpose of the round—to establish equivalence. A clear choice by the facilitator is usually the most effective.

In the course of considering a proposal, rounds dominate with occasional open discussion. In open discussion, the facilitator keeps a mental queue of which person wants to speak next. If the queue becomes too long to remember, this a good indication that a round may be needed. Free form, open discussion can have the advantage of allowing ideas to build quickly. It has the limiting disadvantage that certain personalities may dominate, unbalancing the equivalence that is crucial to the self-organizing process.

In a circle meeting, rounds balance discussion and ensure that everyone has an opportunity to speak. In addition, they make it clear that each person is expected to participate in the deliberations.

Opening Rounds

The sociocratic meeting format both produces and contains the heat of chaos. The opening round creates energy in the room and is very important as the first action of a meeting because the meeting then belongs to each person in the room. When asked to speak to a group about sociocracy, the authors find that the person hosting the presentation often wants to begin with an introduction, despite our request to start with an opening round. The host might say, "Thank you all for coming today to hear John Buck. John lives in Silver Spring, Maryland and has such and such background, etc." The underlying message of such an introduction is (1) I, the person introducing John, am in charge here, and (2) the aim of our gathering is to learn from John.

This undercuts the very basis of sociocratic governance. And it drains energy. We would rather the host let us start with an opening round and save announcements until after the round. If the audience is completely unfamiliar with sociocracy, we (or the host, if knowledgeable) might give a short definition of opening round and then pick someone to start.

The opening round establishes several things:

1. "We the people" gathered here are collectively in charge.
2. We want to develop by working together.
3. We want to attune to each other.

In an opening round, each person will share their uppermost concerns of the moment, particularly in respect to the aim of the circle. People change between meetings, so re-connection is an important need. In the terminology of recent scientific studies, an opening round expands members "zone of alignment" from their immediate co-workers to all the members of the circle and is critical to self-organizing behavior in animal groups (Couzin 2005, 2006; Karreich, 2006).

What people choose to share in an opening round may be work or non-work related. Sometimes a member will pass, sometimes with an attitude that suggests significant fears, frustrations, or anger. It is important that the circle respect the person's right to silence.

Consent Decisions

The process for reaching consent varies depending on the matter at hand. In a simple decision where objections are unlikely, the facilitator may simply make a proposal and ask "any objections?" In others, a complex or controversial policy, for example, the circle may delegate the proposal writing process to a helping circle and then take several meetings and many consent rounds to reach a decision. Most will fall somewhere in between, being resolved in one or two circle meetings with some work outside the meeting to research alternatives.

To reduce meeting time, a well-disciplined circle distributes reports, policy proposals, and descriptions of issues to be discussed and the members read them before the meeting. That way, the facilitator can simply refer to the item and, for example, ask, "Are there any clarifying questions about the latest income statement?" rather than taking time to have the income statement presented. Many decisions will also be made this way, with the facilitator asking for objections, because previous discussion has taken place or it is a routine decision with no new complications.

In some cases, a problem or an issue needs discussion before a proposal can be written. Sometimes a proposal will be written in the meeting, and in other cases, a helping circle will complete it outside the meeting and bring it back to a later meeting for consent.

It is also possible, however, to come to a meeting with an unannounced proposal or to develop a proposal from the information provided in a report, such as the treasurer's report.

Presenting the Proposal

The facilitator asks the person responsible for the agenda item to present the proposal. If the proposal has been distributed before the meeting the presentation may be a simple summary. The circle might want to set rules about circulating proposals at least a week before the circle meeting. That way, people can contact the proposal writer before the meeting with clarifying questions, thus taking up less meeting time.

Preparation is key to achieving consent on more complex or work process altering proposals. For example, if the general circle of a nursing home is proposing to shift from recording patient care notes in a handwritten log to a computer, it would be a good idea for the person presenting the proposal to spend time before the meeting talking with staff to explain how the proposed new system would work.

Clarifying Questions

After the proposal is presented, the facilitator asks if anyone has clarifying questions or, if the proposal is complex, she can ask for questions in a round. As participants ask clarifying questions, the facilitator should ask anyone who starts to express their opinions to "hold that for the moment until we are sure everyone is clear on the proposal." At this point, we just want to make sure that each person has seen or heard the same words and grasps the proposal—at least its basic points.

Quick Reaction Rounds

After a proposal is presented and clarified, the facilitator calls for quick reactions, usually in a round in which members of the circle give short responses to indicate their opinions and reactions to the proposal. "Quick" does mean quick. We encourage people to keep their comments to a few words. Whatever their reaction, it helps if the circle members follow their reactions with *because*, "I like this because..." or "I don't think this will work because..." or "It seems like a workable proposal except it should say something about...."

The purpose of the reaction round is to improve the proposal. If the proposal has obvious flaws, these can be identified in a reaction round without taking much discussion time and the facilitator can suggest that the proposal be referred back for more work.

Often during the reaction round, the person who presented the proposal thinks of a way to make it clearer. For example, if the proposal is that cats and dogs are prohibited in the office, and somebody mentions seeing-eye dogs, the proposal might be re-worded to say that no cats or dogs are allowed in the office with the exception of working dogs. In other cases, the facilitator may choose to assist the proposal maker by suggesting amendments to the proposal.

Ideas expressed in the reaction round often build on each other. If an important new idea bubbles up toward the end of the round, the facilitator can repeat the round to give all circle members an opportunity to react to this information.

A reaction round may occasionally be followed by open discussion in which those with the strongest concerns can share them with the proposal makers. Generally, however, the facilitator will work with the proposer, suggesting the changes that need to be made in the proposal.

Consent Round

Once the proposal is clear and any necessary amendments are made, the facilitator announces a consent round. Working with the secretary to revise the proposal, if necessary, the facilitator asks the secretary to read the proposal and then asks each member of the circle in turn if he or she has any paramount objections to the proposal. The facilitator should proceed to the consent round even if she thinks there will be objections because the objections will be helpful in identifying the most essential issues.

As in opening rounds, the facilitator selects a person at a varying point in the circle to begin, saying, "[Name] we'll begin with you."

During the round the facilitator may ask a person with objections to summarize their objection in a sentence or two. In the nursing home computer example, one circle member might say that he is not able to type and might continue to explain that he can hunt and peck a bit, but it takes a long time.

In consent rounds, objections are not only welcome but sought out. They are not considered barriers to moving forward but opportunities to resolve problems before they obstruct the execution of a policy. If the circle is trying to develop a system that will effectively meet its aim, the circle needs to know if something is wrong with that proposed system. A skilled facilitator, observing a participant say "no objection" with a shrug during the consent round might note the shrug as an objection and say "Jerry, I'm concerned about your shrug. I'll note it as an objection and come back to you."

As in reaction rounds, the facilitator should not allow any discussion of an objection or ask for any details until the consent round has completed and all objections are noted. If no one voices an objection, the facilitator says something like, "Since there are no objections, we have completed that decision" or even "Let's celebrate!"

An issue may need multiple consent rounds if it involves complex or controversial issues. If there are objections, the facilitator has several tools to address them.

Improving the Proposal & Resolving Objections

Once the consent round is complete, any objections can be addressed. Experienced groups can often reach consent more easily than new groups but, of course, some issues are just difficult, even for experienced groups. Multiple rounds and improvements may be needed for some proposals. Some of the more common methods a facilitator might use to resolve objections are to:

- Suggest an amendment to the proposal based on his or her own judgement
- Conduct a round asking, "How might we resolve this?"
- Conduct a brief dialogue between 2-3 people
- Conduct free form discussion on an amendment
- Refer the objection to a subgroup or to a higher circle

Resolving an objection is always an interesting process. Sometimes it is challenging, with heavy tension; sometimes there's lots of laughter. A circle with a little training and experience can resolve its objections. An experienced circle can resolve objections more quickly and easily.

It is important to remember that as soon as a member of the circle makes an objection, it belongs to the whole circle, not just to the person who voiced the objection. An objection is saying, "We have a system for accomplishing our aim, and something isn't working or wouldn't work if we make a change." To use a mechanical systems analogy, if a spark plug of a lawn mower is full of gunk, it will register an "objection" because gunk prevents it from making sparks. It isn't in disagreement with the rest of the lawn mower, it just cannot respond to the operator's attempt to start the mower. The source of the problem is not the spark plug. Spark plugs do not produce gunk. Systems analysis is needed to find the cause of the gunk. Perhaps the underlying cause is a dirty oil filter. Or a loose crankcase. Whatever the problem, the answer is somewhere other than the spark plug.

Thus, in human systems, an objection requires thinking about the whole system. Humans, of course, are a lot more complicated than spark plugs, but we do get "gunky" and the principle is still the same—troubleshooting involves everyone in the system. Thus, in very practical terms, everyone "owns" the objection.

Taking the approach that an objection, once voiced, becomes the property of the whole circle encourages all members of the circle to feel empathy for the objector, a condition that greatly facilitates group problem solving.

Closing Round

Circle meetings end with a closing round that may address issues that were unresolved in the meeting, sometimes an individual has an issue they would like to share, but usually it is an evaluation of the meeting. There is a tendency for people first learning the sociocratic meeting process to make general comments such as "felt nice, we did a lot, enjoyed the company, long and boring, etc." What are needed are specific comments such as "If we'd all read such and such document before the meeting, the *xyz* decision would have been a lot easier," or "We all need to arrive a few minutes early so we can start on time; today we got started 15 minutes late," or "so and so's comment about *xyz* matter was very helpful — it made the issues so much clearer and, facilitator, you picked up on the comment and led us on to a quick decision."

Evaluative comments will vary with the kind of group. A group focused on more personal matters will expect comments like "I feel better after this meeting, more like I belong in this group" or "This discussion of meal planning really cleared the air for me." Sometimes the comments may be more like "I don't feel comfortable when we rush through so many items in one meeting. Perhaps some of them could be handled another way so we have more time for listening to other ideas."

A facilitator preparing to lead a meeting should always look at the closing comments from the previous few meetings. It's very helpful for doing better on the new meeting. For example, given the comments in the previous paragraph, the facilitator might ask the note taker, when sending out the agenda, to remind people to arrive a bit early.

Closing rounds may trigger a desire for ritual. Some circles like to conclude the closing round with a moment of silence to create a transition from the formality of the meeting just as others like to open the meeting with a moment of silence.

The process of conducting consent rounds may seem complicated but the following example, "Sarah's Story," illustrates how easily the process produces good decisions when used by an experienced facilitator.

Additional Resources:

Appendix F, "A Guide for Circle Meetings"

Sara's Story

Consent Decision-Making to the Rescue
By Tena Meadows O'Rear

The following story shows how sociocratic principles and methods can be used by an experienced facilitator even when the group has little knowledge of sociocracy and is not organized sociocratically.

Sara had worked for a few weeks as a consultant to a residential school for emotionally disturbed children, focusing on ways to help the school improve its operations related to safety. A professional facilitator and former mental health worker and administrator, Sara had had training in the sociocratic circle-organization model as part of her work in founding a model community. Sara was facilitating a tense meeting of about 20 persons including staff, the school director, and other school executives, to discuss closing the crisis-stabilization unit and decentralizing the provision of crisis services. The current crisis-stabilization staff would be reassigned to other residential units to provide support in situ, and the former crisis-stabilization unit would be turned into a regular dormitory for boys. This recommendation was made by a task force consisting of staff members across the organization who had analyzed safety concerns in the crisis unit.

The general staff morale was low. Many workers felt that the administration was arbitrary and hypocritical, espousing staff inclusion in decisions but in reality ignoring staff. The director felt frustrated with the staff's constant complaining and felt that several members were only marginally competent.

Crisis in the Meeting

Many meeting participants had opinions about this decision, some on subject, and some wandering off subject and nearly disintegrating into bickering about the reasons why the unit was failing. Everyone agreed that the current unit was not safe. One therapist was particularly opposed to the proposal because she thought that they needed an additional unit for girls much more than an additional unit for boys. The director of admissions was also concerned about closing the unit because it might affect the school's admissions, limiting the school to children with less acute needs.

Then, some of the participants started saying that they should defer the decision, and Sara realized she had to act. It had taken days to coordinate schedules and set up the meeting, and she needed a decision now, not four weeks from now. She hadn't planned to introduce sociocratic methods to the school, but here was a situation crying out for a consent decision.

Mini-Training on Consent

"Actually we can make a decision today," she asserted firmly. She could see several people exchanging amused, sardonic looks. They clearly expected her to fail. "I am going to give you a crash course on the decision-making methodology that we will use. The process I'll describe follows a specific procedure using 'consent.' That sounds like consensus but it's not. One consents to a decision if it is within your range of tolerance. Let me give you a very simple example of what I mean by 'range of tolerance.' When I shop for clothes, I'm likely to pick a blue or green because those colors go well with my complexion. For variety, I might pick out purple, red, or even orange. But yellow is outside my range of tolerance because I look downright sick in yellow." The room began to relax a little.

"Let me give you a more serious example," she continued. "I enjoy relaxed, informal conversation with people, but I can also tolerate formal rituals on the one hand or bawdy locker room banter on the other hand. What I object to, what I cannot tolerate is angry shouting, hitting or humiliating, prejudicial statements of disrespect." Sara could see several nods of agreement.

"What I'm going to do now is ask each of you in turn whether you can consent to the proposal to close the crisis-stabilization unit. In other words, is this proposal within your range of tolerance? The question is not whether this is your favorite direction, but whether you can live with it. If the decision is not within your range of tolerance, I will ask you to explain to us why it is not, i.e. what are your objections. So I'm not seeking your agreement, but rather seeking your objections."

First Consent Round

She picked out one of the people in the room and asked, "George, do you object to the proposal to close the crisis stabilization unit, provide decentralized crisis services, and reopen the unit as a regular residential unit for boys?"

A few people in the room shifted nervously.

"No," answered George.

"Margaret, any objections?" Sara asked the young social worker sitting next to George.

"No objection," Margaret said quietly.

The next three people also consented to the proposal. Then it was the therapist's turn. "Well, I have an objection," she said with folded arms. "I'm fine with the part about closing the crisis stabilization unit; but I think it should be reopened as a regular unit for girls. We already have two girls on the waiting list, and I think we never have enough beds for all the female referrals. Besides without an additional unit for girls, I don't have many choices regarding the mix of girls who reside in each unit, while the boys' therapists have opportunities to mix and match boys already." Sara reflected the part of the proposal that the therapist found acceptable, and the objection, and wrote the objection on the flip chart. She continued around the circle. No objections were raised until the Admissions Director stated that she objected strongly because she thought that admissions would become limited to those children with less acute needs. She suggested that if there were no in-house crisis unit, more hospitalizations would result. Furthermore, she stated that the guidelines for hospitalization were already fuzzy from her perspective.

"Now hold up," the director erupted, "That's not true. The state has clear guidelines about...."

"John," Sara said interrupting the director, "under the process I'm following we don't discuss the objections until we've heard from everyone." He acquiesced and she breathed an inward sigh of relief. It was a gamble to try this process without first training the participants. She turned and noted the objections on the flip chart.

Continuing around the room, she said to the next person, "Barbara, do you have any objections to the proposal?" Everyone else consented to the proposal, with several people throwing in statements of strong support because a regular boys unit represented greater overall safety.

Creative Thinking about the Girls' Needs

Sara said to the group, "Good. We've completed a first round. It's very important to know that two of us would find the proposal intolerable. Returning to the therapist's objection, she asked for more information. The therapist gave an example of a situation where two girls on the same dorm had a hostile relationship that had erupted in a fight. She had no other dorm to use to separate the girls, so she had moved the most volatile girl to the crisis unit. "Without that option, I would have been stuck with no other way to separate them until we could work it out." Two other people in the group chimed in with plausible alternate solutions, including bringing crisis intervention services to the girls' dorm to mediate the conflict on the spot. A second suggestion was to use a vacant extra bed, reserved for guests and rarely used, to serve as a 'cooling off' area for the girls. Mulling over these ideas, the therapist became somewhat enthused about the more flexible approach to crisis intervention, and stated that if those supports were in place, she would not have an objection to the proposal. She ended by emphasizing that she would still rather have another girls dorm, but that she could live with the proposal.

Creative Thinking about the State Guidelines

"Now let's focus on the hospitalization concerns," said Sara. Turning to the director she said, "John, would you share your thoughts about these?"

The director talked for a few moments about the existence of state guidelines for referring the children for psychiatric care. He declared that he couldn't understand why any concern about guidelines should hold up the decision to close down the crisis-stabilization unit.

Sara then asked the Admissions Director who explained that referrals to the crisis unit had been informal because the unit was under school control and located on the school's grounds, and didn't represent a discharge from the school. Yes, there are state guidelines, but they didn't address the specifics of the school's situation: insurance criteria, transportation arrangements, liability and so forth. The finance manager said she was particularly concerned about the lack of clear internal criteria for making the judgment calls necessary to initiate hospitalization.

Sara then asked, "would you be able to live with this proposal if it were modified to include an ad hoc committee consisting of you, the Medical Director, and Director of Clinical Services to produce initial guidelines by Thursday two weeks from today?"

"In that case, I could live with it," responded the Admissions Director. Sara then outlined a process for publishing draft guidelines, soliciting comments from other staff and finalizing the guidelines based on comments. Then she restated the modified proposal with the addition of the guideline work.

Second Consent Round: Decision Made

Sara conducted a second round. The round moved quickly, with each person indicating no objections. After the last person had shaken his head to indicate no objection, Sara said cheerfully, "Good work, everyone! We've all just made an important decision."

There were pleasant looks on many faces. John, the director, spontaneously said, "This is great!" After a minute or two of detailing the process on guideline consideration, the librarian raised her hand. With a puzzled look on her face, she asked, "So, when will the decision be final? In the past we've had meetings like this and thought we made decisions, then the Executive Committee changes them."

Sara explained, "The decision is final. The Executive Committee was here, and they all consented. That's it." The Executive Committee members nodded their concurrence.

Another person said, "I hope you'll tell us more about your process. We have never come to decisions this crisply."

CHAPTER ELEVEN

Electing People

The principle of electing people by consent after open discussion is a logical extension of the general principle of consent, but it is a separate governing principle because the process is both unique and essential to sociocratic functioning. In sociocratic organizations, people are elected to functions and tasks by consent in an open nominations process that includes a final consent round. While people may nominate themselves, volunteering is not accepted because it short-circuits the election process. This process builds a strong sense of trust and ensures that people who assume jobs know they have the support of their peers. Circle members are more likely to trust someone whom they have elected. It also makes day-to-day leadership and decision making much easier because it reduces the friction that results in both autocratic and democratic people selection processes.

Sociocratic elections are usually fun and after the decision, there is often a feeling of quiet satisfaction. This feeling is in contrast to democratic elections, in which the majority is celebrating while the minority may be grieving or fuming, and to autocratic choices in which the boss makes an announcement that may induce feelings of resentment, alienation, jealousy—or even incredulousness.

In the sociocratic process, all members of the circle will have a clear understanding of why each person was chosen and what will be expected of them.

The Election Process

Every one or two years, usually as part of the implementation of the strategic plan, or as otherwise necessary, the circle will meet to elect its members to circle offices and to operational functions and tasks within its domain of responsibility. This may be done in a regular meeting if only one to two people are to be elected or in a meeting devoted to elections if there are a number of positions to be filled or reconfirmed.

The process is the same for each function or task. Circle members consent to a job description, make nominations, give arguments in support of their nominations, make changes based on the arguments presented, and end with a consent round.

Description of the Function or Task

The election process begins with a description of the function or task to be performed—the job. A job description should include the duties, responsibilities, skills and knowledge required, how performance will be reviewed, and the term. Just as no policy should be adopted for an unlimited period, no one should be elected to a job for an unspecified amount of time.

The job can relate to any "doing" task or a function within a circle. For example, in Charles' office, the Marketing Department decided to have large booths at two new professional conventions and assigned the publicity unit to design and set up booths. Susan, operational leader of the Publicity Unit and Charles' supervisor, called a special circle meeting in which Charles was elected to lead the project. The circle also temporarily assigned some of Charles' duties to other members of the circle to free up his time.

Sometimes describing the job is easy. If the task to be assigned is to "research the city laws concerning waste disposal and report back in a month," that may be a sufficient description. The term of service, in this case, is obviously one month, and one criteria for success is obvious: Was the report received in one month? Other times the job may be very complex. When a growing software company's general circle decided that it needed a full-time quality control manager, for example, they began their task description by using Carnegie Mellon University's Configuration Maturity Model before they detailed the tasks related to the job. Since they were not sure how long this job would be useful or whether they had captured everything in their description, they decided to make the term only one year with continuation contingent on evaluation and redefinition. For complex task descriptions like this, the full process of proposal development, reaction rounds, clarification, and consent rounds should be used. (See Chapter Ten, "Consent & Rounds.")

Defining a job is important not only to ensure that the necessary work is done, but also to make sure that its benefit can be properly measured and evaluated. The job description is also a basis for planning the circle's ongoing development program, thus ensuring that each member of the circle has the skills necessary to do the tasks for which they are responsible now and in the future.

Nominations and "Why?"

Once the job description is completed, the secretary hands out small pieces of paper to be used as nomination forms. Pages from small memo pads or index cards work well for this. Nominations for positions are normally done one at a time, in an agreed upon order.

Each circle member, including the facilitator, nominates themselves, someone else, or writes "no nomination" or "hire from outside." A typical completed nomination form will simply say, for example, "Marc nominates Nancy."

The participants then pass the forms to the facilitator. The facilitator stacks the nominations in as-received order, reads the first form out loud, and asks the nominator to explain why they nominated their candidate. "Marc, you nominated Nancy because.....?" Many people are surprised to be nominated and are usually pleased by what people say about their skills. It is a particularly enjoyable part of the process.

As the nominations are read, the facilitator may sort them into piles to keep track of the nominations more easily, but the number of nominations received does not determine the election results. The election is determined by the arguments given for the nominations.

Changes or Amendments

After all circle members have explained their nominations, the facilitator starts a change round by asking, "Would anyone like to change their nomination based on the arguments we've heard? Linda, let's begin with you."

Some may change their nominations to support another nominee, or they may want to add more information in support of their nominee. Some one who originally did not make a nomination may now like to add one. In each case, the facilitator requests a rationale, a "because...." In this process, participants occasionally ask questions of potential candidates or provide clarifying information about themselves.

Consent

Once the nominations have been explained, and some perhaps have changed, the facilitator proposes the person receiving the strongest arguments for the position and gives a rationale for doing so: "I propose Charles for this position. The arguments that Robert and Linda made concerning the recent training he's taken plus his skill with numbers make him particularly well suited. Are there any paramount objections to Charles for this position?" The facilitator then begins a consent round designating a person to start. It is helpful to start the round with the person sitting next to the person nominated so that the person nominated speaks last. The facilitator asks the nominee for his or her objection last so they have full information about the views of the rest of the circle before they respond.

If there are objections, the facilitator asks for the rationale, the "because...." There is no discussion before the consent round is completed.

Objections are resolved using the same process outlined in Chapter Ten, "Consent and Rounds." One choice to resolve an objection is to nominate another person. Another choice is to change the function or task description to meet the proposed candidate's objections. For example, "Can we make this a three-month position instead of a six-month?" or "I'd feel much better if the job description specifically said it wouldn't be necessary for me to consult all members of the circle before finishing. That way I could finish more quickly."

If no one can fill the position, the facilitator declares a vacancy and asks the operational leader to take the initiative to fill it from outside the circle in accordance with the circle's hiring policy. This may require budget approval from a higher circle.

When objections seem to have been resolved, possibly resulting in an amended job description or a decision to conduct an outside search, the facilitator does a final consent round to confirm the decision.

Precautions

It is important to *avoid* asking before the process begins who is interested, or not interested in the position. The election process belongs to the circle, not to individual members. In many cases once the circle has presented its reasons for choosing a specific person, that person is more likely to accept the election. If the proposed person finds it impossible to accept, it may be clearer how the task description could be amended.

A second reason to avoid asking who is willing to serve is that the person who volunteers for a position may not be suitable. Once a person volunteers it is hard to reverse the process and ask for nominations. When the process begins with nominations and everyone hears the arguments for them, it becomes more obvious who is most qualified for the position and unqualified people will not be put forward, by themselves or others.

As in any other round, during the presentations round, in which people give arguments in favor of those they have nominated, there should be no discussion. It is important that the round be completed and all views shared before they are discussed.

Objecting to a proposed person should never provide an excuse for an attack. The facilitator should stop any attempt to label someone and help the objector formulate their objection, for example, in terms of the needs of the objector that would not be met if the proposed person were elected. In this way, it is possible to keep the focus of the election on the aim of the circle. Remember that no candidate is perfect; it is always more or less.

Finally, be sure to specify a term for the function or task. This makes it much easier to evaluate and change the incumbent if necessary.

Let the Process Work

It is important to follow this process precisely because the elements of a system must be equivalent if they are to self-organize. Having each person write their opinion separately on a nomination form creates a situation in which many possibilities are present, and one in which no one's opinion is influencing others. The change round creates an additional opportunity for self-organization.

When first encountering this process, some express concern about the power of the facilitator. The facilitator, for example, is free to propose someone with fewer nominations than another person. But in sociocracy, plurality is not a decisive factor; it is only one of the arguments to consider. The circle elects the facilitator, in part, for their ability to listen and to make sound judgments.

If a member of the circle objects to the facilitator's proposal, they may object and present different arguments during the consent round. Allowing the facilitator to quickly propose what appears to be the most workable choice moves the circle forward, and the consent round ensures that the choice is within the circle's range of tolerance. This practice both encourages strong leadership and provides a process for correcting an error in judgment.

Other Decisions

The election process is actually a special application of the principle of consent and can be used to make any decision in which there are a discrete number of choices. The date of a holiday party, for example, or the location of the next conference. (For other uses of the election process, see Romme 2000, 2003.)

Additional Resources:

Appendix I, "Guide to Elections by Consent"

CHAPTER TWELVE

Organizing Work
by Producing Organization

☙❦❧

We easily recognize the phrase "organizing production," meaning to design a process for producing a product or providing a service to a customer. The reverse is not so familiar, "producing organization." Producing organization is a very important concept in sociocratic organizations. It refers to planning all the processes that will form and guide the organization in doing its work. A poor process will have a negative effect regardless of how skillful the leader is or how much money is spent implementing it. As noted earlier, a four-wheel car with one wheel missing will be difficult to drive, despite the capabilities of the driver or the quality of the other three wheels.

In addition to designing organizations that "have all their wheels," sociocratic methods focus on designing organizations that thrive in changing environments. To use the car analogy again, if you need to drive over bumpy roads, you will need shock absorbers not just to keep the passengers comfortable but to protect the engine parts from vibrations and jolts. Motors, like people, work better with less friction. For the car to operate in changing temperatures, it needs fluids that flow when it is cold and do not combust or evaporate when it is hot.

Like automobiles, sociocratic organizations are designed to function in changing conditions. Unlike automobiles, however, organizations need to adjust to *unforeseen* changing conditions. Like deer avoiding a predator, they need to be able to sense changes in the environment and adapt quickly. An organization needs to be designed *and redesigned*—and it has to keep functioning while being redesigned. Like the deer that needs to avoid its predators, it also needs to eat. Similarly, the organization must be able to function and adapt at the same time. To achieve the dual goals of functioning and adapting, the sociocratic organization needs processes for change as well as for production, to produce organization on a monthly and sometimes even a daily basis, not just once at inception.

Producing organization is one of the chief activities of a circle. Just as everyone in most offices now has basic computer skills, in sociocratic offices everyone needs organization-engineering skills. Such skills used to be limited to industrial engineers and management consultants. Today they are the responsibility of leadership—and in a sociocratic organization *everyone* is responsible for leadership.

While all the principles and methods used in sociocratic organizations support the process of producing organization, designing the work process is most specifically related. In Chapter Five, "Developing Quality," we presented the steps in producing organization and discussed vision and mission in some detail. While remembering that aims exist in the context of visions and missions, we will focus here on the aim, the production and steering process, and the program of ongoing development. These steps repeated from Figure 5.3 are:

Define a Vision
Define a Mission
Define an Aim
Design a Production Process
Design a Steering Process
Determine Task Division and Delegation
Design a Program of Ongoing Development

Defining an Aim

The three elements of a good aim statement are:

(1) A named product or service that

(2) Is differentiated from other aims, and

(3) Described in terms your customer or client understands.

A well-defined aim attracts clients and prevents us from working at cross-purposes. Part of producing organization is designing the cir-

Figure 12.0

EXAMPLES OF AIMS
IN THE CONTEXT OF THEIR VISIONS & MISSIONS

Organic Gardener

Vision: Organic, inexpensive vegetables on the family table all year.

Mission: Plant a garden large enough to provide vegetables all year.

Aim: Fresh vegetables in summer; canned and frozen in winter.

Roaming Computer Services for a Large Company

Vision: Every employee has access to all the information they need to do their work 24 hours a day, 7 days a week, anywhere in North America.

Mission: To provide remote access to all company data, while providing appropriate security protection to each piece of data.

Aim: Laptops to all employees who travel and a portal screen linked to satellite internet services.

City Fire Department

Vision: A city with no deaths by fire; annual per incident losses lowest in the nation.

Mission: Build an outstanding fire safety infrastructure.

Aim: Staffed and equipped fire stations within 10 minutes of all houses. All ages trained in fire safety. Fire drills in all schools and businesses. Regular building inspections.

Spring Manufacturer

Vision: People riding comfortably in cars, even on bumpy roads.

Mission: Provide high-quality springs for shock absorbers to car manufacturers.

Aim: Springs of gauges x, y, and z; a full range of tensile strengths.

Hospital

Vision: An area of the city in which everyone has immediate access to high quality inpatient health care.

Mission: Provide health care in a warm and caring environment that supports patients and their loved ones physically, emotionally, intellectually and spiritually.

Aim: Emergency services for acute trauma or illness; in-patient services that allow family visits 20 hours per day; and in-person on-site access to trained spiritual advisors and counselors 24 hours a day, 7 days a week, for all patients and family members.

cular process, the leading-doing-measuring. Thus a well-formulated aim is a prerequisite for designing a good process. To be effective, you need to know where you are going.

"A Named Product or Service"

One good test of whether you've actually written a clear aim is to ask yourself the questions, "Could I buy one? Or hire it? Or use it? Or enjoy it?" For example, if someone says, "My aim is to change the world," we would ask, "Can I buy three changed worlds? Deliver them tomorrow!" Obviously, a changed world is not a description of a product or service. To change the world could be your vision, but an aim is something you can exchange with someone. You have to be able to produce it.

We make many exchanges everyday. We give the grocer money and the grocer gives us vegetables. We watch the neighbors' dog when they are on vacation with the expectation that they will watch our cats when we go on vacation. We go to work in exchange for a salary. We also do many things for others for which we do not expect anything in exchange, because we receive something from ourselves—self-respect or pride in our work. This is also an exchange.

The objective of an aim statement is to define the product or service that has exchange value.

Creating an exchange means both making and then keeping an agreement with a client. In defining the work process, producing organization, you must be able to define how you will:

(1) negotiate an exchange with your client,

(2) create the product or service, and

(3) make the exchange.

In writing an aim, listen to your customers or clients and, if possible, your potential customers or clients. What do they say about their needs in relationship to your area of expertise? What product would fulfill those needs? Does it exist? The old adage "Before you build a better mouse trap, find out if there are any mice" is a good one to judge whether there is an opportunity for exchange.

Once you determine that there is an opportunity for an exchange, that a product or service is needed and that you can provide it, the next step is to write your aim statement. Be as objective and factual as possible. Saying "Our aim is to make exciting new ergonomic chairs that will ease many people's back pains" is to state an aim with a story added. If you say, "Our aim is to make ergonomic chairs that ease back pains," you are stating your aim more clearly.

"Differentiated from Other Aims"

How does your ergonomic chair differ from other chairs, particularly from other ergonomic chairs. What is your market niche? For example, if you say, "Our aim is to manufacture plastic ergonomic chairs for the elderly population in the northeastern United States," your statement is more focused and more distinguished from other aims of other organizations. This both focuses the steering of your organization and opens possibilities for exchanges with organizations working with the elderly and in the northeastern United States.

Aims rarely exist solely in themselves. Aims are often sub-aims of a larger aim. Thus, the aim of one section of a department store might be "to provide children's clothing" but it would be defined in the context of the store's overall aim "to provide affordable consumer household goods." A rubber producer might have an aim that is not just to produce rubber but to produce rubber for a specific industry. This would determine, for example, whether the rubber producer would make its product in huge quantities or in smaller quantities. A theater might produce plays but do it in the context of a civic aim to improve arts education in urban neighborhoods. This would be a very different aim than if they were producing plays in a large Broadway theater.

"Described in Terms Your Customer or Client Understands"

The aim should use language that your customer or client understands. In our example of Charles' software company, if his company has developed a new game that introduces five-year-old children to mathematics, he would not use highly technical computer programming language on the package. If his aim is to produce a product that will be attractive and useful to parents who purchase software in toy departments, he must describe his product in language they understand. On the other hand, if his company is designing software for an advanced school system network, he must use language that would make his product attractive to information technology experts working for the school system.

Designing the Production Process

The next step in producing organization is to determine how you will fulfill your aim. How will you market, produce, and deliver your product? Designing the *doing* in a sociocratic organization requires laying out all the steps necessary to produce the product or service described in your aim.

Creating a product or service requires finding clients, changing assets (money, materials, skills, etc.) into something new (product or service), and then providing it to clients. This process, as do all processes, has three components: *input-transformation-output*. *Input* is your agreement with your customers. You *transform* the money, materials, skills, and other assets into a product or service, and then *output* them to a customer or client. *Output* includes receiving compensation and completes the exchange process.

Steering input-transformation-output step requires a circular process: leading, doing, and measuring. Input, for example, requires an acquisition plan (leading), acquisition activities (doing) and collecting data about the results of the acquisition activities (measuring). The 9-Block Chart in Figure 12.1 illustrates the relationship between input-transformation-output more clearly. It is a grid for designing each step. Figure 12.2 is a completed chart showing the "doing" steps in planning a guest room service. Breaking the process down into smaller and smaller steps creates the basis for job and task descriptions necessary in organizing any work process.

The chart is actually a fractal; it repeats itself in self-similar units at each level of detail. Each of the nine blocks in the chart describes one of the three steps of input, transformation, output associated with one of the three parts of the circular process—leading, doing, and measuring. Each of these parts can likewise be expanded into a three step input-transformation-output process, producing a chart with 27 blocks. The process of developing a long format proposal for consent is presented in Appendix F, "Guide for Circle Meetings," and illustrates how proposal development follows this process. The information gathering process, or "picture forming," is the input, proposal development is the transformation, and consent to a final version is the output. It is useful to analyze any process using the input-transformation-output paradigm.

Typically, organizations focus on and develop the middle block, doing/transforming, and neglect to organize and document the other eight blocks. For example, the authors are aware of a software development company certified at a high level in the Configuration Maturity Model quality standard for software development that has a sales force with no common database of sales contacts and few contacts on the marketing and sales process.

A strong organization will plan and articulate each step—each block—of the producing organization process in detail.

Adding the Steering Wheel: Leading and Measuring

In designing a work process, it is generally easiest to articulate the doing steps for producing the aim first. Once these steps are defined, the next step in producing organization is to add the leading and measuring steps. Once you have determined what you are going to do (the doing), you decide how you are going to do it (the leading) and what data you need if you are going in the right direction (the measuring). This is the circular process of leading-doing-measuring presented in Chapter Seven, "New Leadership Strategies."

Leading

Unpredictable events, disturbances, will occur as we pursue our aims. The purpose of leadership is to steer us through or around those disturbances. Without disturbances, we could organize our work processes just once and function robotically without a leader. In robotic world everyone shows up for work on time and never takes more than the allotted time for lunch. This is the world that strict, static autocratic organizations pretend they inhabit. But in most work environments, life is not so predictable. It is the task of the operational leader to make the moment-to-moment decisions that are necessary when things do not go as planned. Thus, we must be sure that every step in the producing organization process includes a leading function.

Like recognized quality control methods such as ISO 9000, the sociocratic process of producing organization encourages documentation of valid policies so that everyone knows as specifically and reliably as possible what to do.

One measure of the quality of leading is the occurrence of problems. When breakdowns, errors, bickering between coworkers, or other

9-Block Chart Used to Produce Organization and Plan the Exhange Process.-

	Typical Vocabulary	Input Determining the Exchange Relation		Transformation Generating the Exchange Objects		Output The Exchange	
Leading	Set Criteria Create Evaluate Formulate Plan Schedule	**1**	Who:	**4**	Who:	**7**	Who:
Doing	Arrange Organize Provide Maintain Perform	**2**	Who:	**5**	Who:	**8**	Who:
Measuring	Review Record Quantify Verify	**3**	Who:	**6**	Who:	**9**	Who:

Figure 12.1 A 9-Block Chart. Used to produce organization and plan the exchange process, the 9-Block Chart integrates the leading-doing-measuring functions with the input-transformation-output processes.

9-Block Chart for Achieving the Aim of Producing a Guest Room Service.

	Typical Vocabulary	Input	Transformation	Output
Leading	Set Criteria Create Describe Evaluate Formulate Plan Schedule	**1** Describe guest room facilities and services. Formulate budget and procedures for advertising. **Who:** Linda	**4** Create procedures for check-in and staff hiring and training. Plan and schedule room maintenance services. **Who:** Linda	**7** Determine methods and procedures for billing and payment for services. Create methods for encouraging guests to return. **Who:** William
Doing	Arrange Organize Provide Maintain Perform	**2** Advertise and register new guests. **Who:** Sue	**5** Provide services to guests. Decorate and maintain rooms and other facilities. Hire, train, and manage staff. **Who:** Sue	**8** Perform actions required for check out, payment, and checking guest satisfaction. **Who:** George
Measuring	Review Record Quantify	**3** Record how guests learn about the rooms and why they come. **Who:** Sue	**6** Record data on guest interaction, costs, service gaps, etc. **Who:** Sue	**9** Record any problems with checkout Assess guest satisfaction. **Who:** Sue

Figure 12.1 A 9-Block Chart for a Guest Room Service.

trouble situations occur, an effective leader will solve the immediate problem and then ask him- or herself, "In what way did the structure and policies I have established contribute to that problem?" The authors' own experience indicates that troubles on the floor always have some corresponding error or omission in the supervisor's office. So, to produce leading, you must examine your policies every time an anticipated success does not occur.

Measuring

In addition to leading, an essential part of the steering process is measuring. For a cyclist to ride a bicycle she must measure properly. For example, her eyes receive a picture of the environment and her inner ears assess her environment to steer effectively. This principle is true for all work processes. To guide "doing," the cyclist must lead and measure. In order to lead, there must be information available about the effect of doing; there must be measurement. So, each step of the process also has to have a measuring function.

Developing measurement methods is just as challenging as formulating good leading policies. A clumsy measurement process chews up time better spent on other matters. Anyone who has ever completed an order or a sale by filling out voluminous accounting forms knows too well about the potential frustrations of a measurement burden.

To check the quality of your measurement process, ask yourself how well the measurement reflects the processes it is measuring. If you are the captain of a large ship, you want to know how your engine is functioning. You must stay on the bridge and cannot go personally to see the engine; you rely on instruments. One dial shows the pressure in the boiler. Another shows the amount of fuel remaining. Yet another shows the revolutions per minute, and so forth. These dials are quite different physically from the dramatic reality of a loud, hot engine churning. Abstract representation of concrete characteristics is the essence of measuring. Numbers can be analyzed and compared in ways that other information cannot.

Inventing a useful and relevant measurement tool can mean success or failure of a project. The Wright Brothers, for example, managed to invent the airplane before their competitors in part because they invented wind tunnels and other devices to measure lift and steerability.

Allocation of Tasks

We must assign people not only to the doing tasks but to the leading and measurement tasks as well. Typically a person will have a doing function as well as a measurement function or a leading function for other steps. In a sociocratically organized hairdressing shop, for example, clients are received by the receptionist and then handed off to someone who washes their hair in preparation for the hair dressing process. The hair washer washes hair, doing, and is also responsible for measuring the receptionist by asking the client, "Did you get a cup of coffee while you were waiting?" Or, "What do you think of the new décor we have in the waiting area?" After the client moves on, the hair washer takes a moment to jot down feedback from the client on a card. Later in the day, she gives all the cards she has filled out to the person responsibility for setting policy about how clients will be received or how the reception area appears to clients. Thus, in filling out a 9-Block Chart, we would put the hair washer's name in the doing block for hair washing, and in the measurement block for the receptionist's activities and the appearance of the reception area.

Circles can allocate tasks using the election by consent process or delegate task allocation to the operational leader to be assigned in the traditional way. A fully functioning sociocratic organization will usually revise its aim at least every two years, redesign the organization based on the new aim statements, and elect everyone to functions and tasks.

Development

Development is the responsibility of each circle and occurs through researching, learning, and teaching as is appropriate to the needs of the circle. Endenburg recommends that 5% of an organization's resources (time and money) be reserved for development.

Circle members keep their development plans, their individual plans and the larger circle plans, in their personal logbooks.

Why Design Organizations in This Way?

The sociocratic circle-organization model has a number of advantages:

- Complex processes remain steerable.

- Processes do not become isolated from their environment.
- Circle members can see their domain (common aim and process).
- Circle members are made responsible for the results of their circle. That is, "They ought to do such and such..." becomes "We ought..."
- No gaps will occur between two processes. That is, things are less likely to "fall through the cracks."
- Because each process, on every level in the organization, follows the same conceptual model, troubleshooting organizational problems becomes much easier.
- The management and/or information system forms an integral part of the primary production process.
- Orientation towards the client is included in the process.
- Coordination problems between people, which are often due to errors in constructing processes, are lessened.
- Ongoing exchanges remain beneficial to both partners.

Additional Resources:

Appendix F, "Guide for Circle Meetings," includes a brief summary of the steps in producing organization.

CHAPTER THIRTEEN
Money as Measurement

Sociocratic organizations use many kinds of measurement to determine if they are achieving their aims. As we discussed in Chapter Five, "Developing Quality," measurement is the third step in the circular process of leading-doing-measuring that ensures the dynamic performance of a self-correcting, self-optimizing system. While we normally recognize the need for leaders and understand "doing" as essential, we often give little attention to measurement, particularly in non-profit organizations and membership associations. But measurement, as we have seen, is essential to steering a self-organizing system. For people to participate fully in their organizations, they need to be a part of the measuring just as they are part of the leading and doing. They need this feedback, negative or positive, to know whether their actions are effective and to participate as entrepreneurs.

One way to involve all participants in measurement is to provide them with feedback about their own individual and collective performance. In Chapter Eight, "Fair Compensation & Free Organizations," we presented the concepts of profit as measurement and the division of compensation into the fixed Guaranteed Base Wage (GBW) based on the labor market and the variable Short-Term Measurement (STM) and Long-Term Measurement (LTM) based on measured performance. In this chapter we will explain how to calculate these measurements based on profits so that each participant in an organization directly experiences the results of good (or bad) performance.

Retained Reserves

As the first step in planning for the next fiscal year, the top circle reviews and approves the budget proposal by the general circle. The top circle decides how much it wants to add to the company's reserves (or savings) in the coming year. The top circle considers such factors as the organization's current level of reserves, anticipated economic conditions, any anticipated cash flow constraints, planned capital improvements, and so on.

Projected Profit

The next step is for the top circle to set an expected percentage of profit for the company as a whole for the coming year. As with retained reserves, there will be many considerations affecting this decision, including previous years' experience, emergence of new competition, prevailing lending rate (Federal Reserve prime lending rate), anticipated improvements in productivity, etc. For an association, these would include new grants, government programs, donation levels, changing target population needs, etc.

After setting an overall profit rate as a target, the top circle should give guidelines to the general circle for adjusting the expected rate of profit for each department. For example, the top circle may decide to carry a department at a loss or reduced profit to reflect start-up of a new product line or a marketing strategy to fend off competition. If the decision is to reduce the target profit for one department, the other departments will have to make up the difference with higher profit targets.

Chart 13.1, for example, shows three departments of a company. The departments provide various products and services. The top circle of the company set a profit target of 10% for the new fiscal year for the whole company (($8M − 7.2M)/8.00=10%). Because Department A is selling a new product line in a competitive market, that department's expected profit for the year is only 5%. The services provided by Department B are suddenly in high demand, and the top circle and the department believe that a 12% profit is feasible. This higher rate of profit offsets the company's investment in Department A. Department C provides the company's established product line and is expected to have stable profits.

Chart 13.1 Projected Next Year's Profit.

DEPARTMENT	(A) PROJECTED EXPENSES	(B) PROJECTED GROSS REVENUE	(C) PROJECTED % PROFIT ((B – A)/B)
A	$ .95M	$1M	5%
B	$2.65M	$3M	12%
C	$3.60M	$4M	10%
TOTALS	$7.20M	$8M	10%

Company-Wide Weighting Factors

The next step is to calculate company-wide weighting factors, including company reserves, investors, and staff on general overhead, for use in profit distribution. Investment capital is made possible by earlier labor and can be considered as condensed labor. This means that active labor and investment capital are fundamentally similar, and therefore, both can be used in calculating ratios for profit sharing. In other words, $100 in investment capital has the same relative value as $100 of active labor. It can be argued that investment capital should be weighted somewhat higher than active labor because investment capital represents the residue of active labor after taxes. The organization can make such adjustments so long as capital investment and labor are treated as fundamentally similar.

With that concept understood, we can calculate weighting factors and use them to calculate short- and long-term measurements.

For the company reserve, the investors, and employees on general overhead, we calculate weighting factors by dividing the reserve requirement and investor or employee contribution by the last year's gross revenue. For example, the value of the investor's shares at the end of the fiscal year was $1M. The indirect employees' labor contribution was $1.2 million. Assuming that last year's gross revenue was $8M, we calculate the weighting factors shown in Chart 13.2 for use in profit distribution for reserve, investor, and indirect (overhead) staff.

Chart 13.2 Company-Wide Weighting Factors

PARTICIPANT	(A) VALUE OF REQUIRED CONTRIBUTION	(B) LAST YEAR GROSS REVENUE	(C) WEIGHTING FACTOR (A/B)
Company Reserve Requirement Amount set by top circle	$0.5M	$8M	0.06
Investors' market value of shares at end of fiscal year, professional estimate, or book value of company	$1M	$8M	0.13
Staff: Indirect staff base salaries last fiscal year	$1.2	$8M	0.15

Calculating Short-Term Measurement

Chart 13.3 shows an example of calculating Short-Term Measurement. Assume that Department A got a fixed price contract for $50,000. The projected profit from Chart 13.1, calculated into the contract bid, was 5% or $2,500. The work, however, went better than expected; material costs were $22,500, exactly as predicted, but labor costs were only $20,000 rather than $25,000. This savings was achieved, in part, by new work methods developed by the workers Jones, Smith, and Green. Because the actual profit was 15% ($50,000 – $42,500), the company calculates STM as follows.

We will divide the STM among the company reserve, investors, and everyone who directly or indirectly contributed labor to the work. The indirect participants were the company general manager, administrative department (general overhead), and the manager of Department A. Because Department A manager handles several contracts and does not report time by each contract, her contribution is calculated as indirect for purposes of this example.

We calculate the weighting factors for those who contributed direct labor as the ratio of their projected wages to the value of the con-

Chart 13.3 Amount of STM to Be Divided

Amount of Order (Revenue)		$50,000

Cost to fill order:
            Materials
            Labor
	$22,500
	$20,000	

Total Cost		$42,500
Net profit (Revenue – Cost) Less expected profit (5%)		$ 7,500 $ 2,500
Amount of STM to be divided		$ 5,000

tract. The wages were originally estimated at $25,000; thus, the direct labor weighting factor is $25,000/$50,000 = 0.5. We will use this factor along with the factors calculated in Chart 13.2 to calculate the STM for each contributor.

In order to calculate the weighting factors for the individual workers, we subdivide the 0.5 direct labor weighting factor as shown in Chart 13.4. Finally, we calculate each contributor's share of the $5,000 STM as shown in Chart 13.5. Each contributor's STM factor is calculated by dividing the individual weighting factor (A) by the sum of all the weighting factors (Sum A). The dollar amount is derived by multiplying this ratio by $5,000 (column C).

Chart 13.4 Determining Direct Labor Weighting Factors by Individual.

WORKER	(A) ORIGINALLY ESTIMATED HOURS	(B) BASE WAGE RATE	(C) ORIGINALLY ESTIMATED BASE LABOR COST (A*B)	(D) ORIGINALLY ESTIMATED TOTAL CONTRACT VALUE	(E) WEIGHTING FACTOR (C/D)
Jones	200	$40/hr	$8,000	$50,000	0.16
Smith	200	$35/hr	$7,000	$50,000	0.14
Green	500	$20/hr	$10,000	$50,000	0.20

Chart 13.5. Calculation of STM in Dollars Using Weighting Factors in Charts 13.2 and 13.4.

PARTY	(A) WEIGHTING FACTOR	(B) STM CALCULATION FACTOR (A/SUM A)	(C) DOLLAR SHARE OF STM (B*5,000)
Reserve	0.06	0.071	$357.14
Investors	0.13	0.155	$773.81
Indirect Staff	0.15	0.179	$892.86
Jones	0.16	0.190	$952.38
Smith	0.14	0.167	$833.33
Green	0.20	0.238	$1,190.48
SUM	0.84	1.000	$5,000.00

Calculating Long-Term Measurement (LTM)

The $2,500 which represents the earnings from the anticipated 5% profit is divided among the participants using parallel formulas once every six months or a year. At a typical sociocratic organization, the great majority of staff invests some of their savings in the company—essentially like stockholders. In this way, they increase the amount they earn in both the short- and long-term measurement paybacks because they are compensated for their investment of both labor and capital.

Some Effects of the System

Because a company's books are open to all employees, with appropriate safeguards to preserve competitive secrets, this measurement system has proven, over time, to be resistant to tricks and manipulations. The measurement reflects group performance, promoting cooperation while recognizing individual performance.

Compensating the overhead and administrative staff promotes great efficiency instead of the typical attitude of disinterest. For example, the accounting departments are typically rather assertive in collecting outstanding payments since they (nor anyone else) do not receive their STM payment until the money is collected. Further, the sales force has an incentive to maintain communications with the operational staff in order to support them in their work. Unlike the typical arrangement where the sales force gets a percentage of the initial contract value, in a sociocratic organization, part of their income is based on the successful completion of work, not just the initial sale.

A worker who finishes a job in fewer than expected hours is able to go on to other work. The most efficient workers can, therefore, significantly increase their income through STM payments. Over time, the base salaries of such workers may be increased. It is possible, thus, for bright new workers to accelerate increases in their income without having to wait for annual reviews or the judgments of supervisors who may not be as timely or objective. As production increases, the money available for STM payments increases. Increases are driven by performance—both individual and group performance.

What if the profit in our example had been $2,000, only 4%, one percent below the expected 5% profit? That would create an STM deficit. Everyone would have to make up that deficit in the next contract before they could receive any further STM payments. In this way, everyone would feel the effects (the measurement) of less than expected performance.

Using this method, everyone is a partner, and everyone is able to help steer the organization toward fiscal health.

Other Considerations

The measurement system outlined can be applied to nonprofit organizations as well, but the category for investors is not applicable just as it is not applicable for small, unincorporated businesses.

If the nature of an organization's contracts is not fixed fee, provision should still be made for STM/LTM payments. For example, if a contract is cost plus fixed fee, part of the fixed fee can be set aside for the short term measurement. If the contract is purely time and materials, then part of the profit calculation embedded in labor rates should be set aside for STM/LTM payments.

Finally, how can a company use this system in a transparent way without increasing the risk that key financial information will leak to competitors? That is, how can an organization both be transparent and have a black box? Under normal circumstances circles simply accept that sensitive figures such as overhead rates are correctly reflected in calculations of short and long term measurements. If a circle suspects "something funny" in those calculations, however, it can elect a trusted member of its circle to review the accounting books. That member can then report back to the circle that, "Everything is okay."

There are undoubtedly many other possible solutions. This "special eyes" strategy has been used successfully for many years at Endenburg Electrotechniek and other companies.

An Invitation to Share

Sociocracy is, above all, about engaging with one another to achieve our aims. It places power in the hands of those who actively participate in creating organization. We hope the sociocratic principles and methods that we have presented here will help people build the businesses, neighborhoods, communities, and cities they most want, and to develop the structures and governments that will allow us to live more freely and richly with less strife and waste.

In closing, we would like to share some ideas that are still fragmentary and some experiences from recent training. One such experience was reported by a mother preparing her family for a holiday celebration:

> "We had a sociocratic family meeting last week in which we wanted to plan the activities of our Christmas holidays. Because many questions came up in the previous meeting, my family members had requested an introduction to sociocracy. I was facilitating. I did a short presentation, and then we went on with the agenda. Because we were short on time, I made a proposal to form sub-groups for special preparations, for example, one to plan for meals, one to plan for games, etc. In the whole family group, we created a time frame and fixed dates for the small groups to complete their work. The next day we met in a small group for preparation of meals. Elisabeth, age 10, facilitated in the way she had seen me do. She also took notes.

You cannot imagine how quickly children absorb. After this small group, the children met in their sub-group with the intention to prepare games. This time Leonard, age 13, facilitated. I was not a member. That evening, we gathered and Elisabeth and Leonard presented the decisions of the small groups. It was amazing to see this happen."

This is one small example of how sociocratic methods work to help us organize our lives more harmoniously. Both the principles and methods are simple and straightforward enough to be understood by children with little training but the effect is very powerful.

As more organizations adopt sociocracy people will become more connected in supportive ways. For example, in The Netherlands there are circles composed of the general managers from a wide variety of sociocracy organizations in which the managers meet to support each other and share ideas about the application of sociocratic methods. It is possible that some day such circles will evolve into a kind of city-wide general circle. We invite you to participate in this adventure as you develop your own sociocratic groups.

What about society itself? What would it be like to have sociocratic institutions everywhere: the government, schools, theaters, banks, businesses—all coordinated sociocratically? The answer is we do not know. However, work is going forward. For example, in the city of Woerden, in the center of The Netherlands, many neighborhoods and neighborhood centers are organized sociocratically. In Enschede, in the eastern part of The Netherlands, all 30 schools in the public school system function sociocratically. Other promising and more extensive projects are underway, but it is too soon to publish their stories.

Sociocratic thought continues to develop and to spread around the world. This book has focused on the basic theory and its application in the management of business organizations, but there is also a whole other dimension of sociocracy—its vision for society.

For example, consider security. If a modern police department succeeds in reducing crime or reducing auto accidents, who profits? Not the police department but rather the insurance companies. Ironically, it is not in the best interests of the police department to eliminate crime completely. If crime disappeared so would the budget for the police department, because the police depend on criminals for their jobs. Thinking sociocratically, is there another way to pay the police department? For example, could tax money be treated like an insurance payment in which the police, rather than the insurance company, would pay you if your house was robbed? This would make the aim of the police department truly to stop crime because they would profit from less crime, not from more. This is the kind of creative thinking that sociocracy encourages.

Consider health care, for example, a system whose costs are accelerating faster than costs in other parts of society. Under the current medical care system where people pay to be restored to health, is it in a doctor's best interest to have no sick patients? If a doctor has very healthy patients, the insurance company profits, not the doctor. In traditional China, people paid acupuncturists to keep their family healthy. If someone got sick, the acupuncturist would charge nothing. This is truly health care. The aim is to maintain health and to profit from doing so, not to profit from illness.

But health care is intricately intertwined with other parts of society. For example, on-the-job stresses seem to contribute to medical problems. People would likely be healthier if those stresses could be controlled. Looking at problems this way makes us realize how complex society is and how fragmented our means of not only resolving problems but even sharing information about them is. Sociocracy provides a structure for linking organizations in a meaningful way with the potential of addressing such complex and interrelated problems in an integrated way.

If you were trying to apply sociocratic principles in your city or town, how would you go about creating a circle structure? How might a circle structure for an entire region accelerate the development of better ways to organize society? These are still open design questions, and we invite your thoughts.

We are interested to know about your personal story in relation to sociocracy and your responses as you read the book. What caused you to push through to this point? Perhaps you are a business leader looking for ways to make your company more profitable; perhaps a member of a social change organization searching for a way to make your group more effective in harmony with your values; or perhaps you are an law enforcement officer wondering how to organize your department to reduce job stress.

Whatever your perspective, we encourage you to share it with others. You can contact John Buck at Governance Alive:

Telephone at 1-800-870-2092
Email: contact@GovernanceAlive.com
Website: www.governancealive.com

The Governance Alive website is being developed as a clearing house for ideas, offering both informal and structured ways to connect to others who share a curiosity and interest in sociocracy as well as a way to support continuing training and education.

You can contact Sharon Villines through the Sociocracy.info website. Sociocracy.info is a comprehensive information resource about sociocracy including reading lists, links, email discussion lists, and publications.

www.sociocracy.info

We look forward to a more interactive connection with you and joy as we explore together new ways to make our cultures and society as much fun as possible.

APPENDICES

Additional Resources

Sociocracy

Lester Frank Ward (1841-1913)

⟨❧⟩

Frank Ward was a clerk who obtained his college degrees in botany and law by studying evenings. He then worked as a paleontologist and archeologist for the federal government until the age of 65 when he accepted a professorship at Brown University and began a new career. Elected the first president of the International Institute of Sociology in 1903 and first president of the American Sociological Society in 1906, he has been called the Father of American Sociology and America's Aristotle. This selection is from The Psychic Factors of Civilization *was published in 1893.*

The world, having passed through the stages of autocracy and aristocracy into the stage of democracy, has, by a natural selection against personal power, so far minimized the governmental influence that the same spirit which formerly used the government to advance self is now ushering in a fifth stage, that of *plutocracy*, which thrives well in connection with a weak democracy, and aims to supersede it entirely. Its strongest hold is the widespread distrust of all government, and it leaves no stone unturned to fan the flame of misarchy. Instead of demanding more and stronger government it demands less and feebler. Shrewdly clamouring for individual liberty, it perpetually holds up the outrages committed by governments in their autocratic and aristocratic stages, and falsely insists that there is imminent danger of their reënactment. *Laissez faire* and the most extreme individualism, bordering on practical anarchy in all except the enforcement of existing proprietary rights, are loudly advocated, and the public mind is thus blinded to the real condition of things....

The great evils under which society now labors have grown up

181

during the progress of intellectual supremacy. They have crept in stealthily during the gradual encroachment of organized cunning upon the domain of brute force. Over that vanishing domain, government retains its power, but it is still powerless in the expanding and now all-embracing field of psychic influence. No one ever claimed that in the trial of physical strength the booty should fall to the strongest. In all such cases the arm of the government is stretched out and justice is reinforced. But in those manifold, and far more unequal struggles now going on between mind and mind, or rather between the individual and an organized system, the product of ages of thought, it is customary to say that such matters must be left to regulate themselves, and that the fittest must be allowed to survive. Yet, to anyone who will candidly consider the matter, it must be clear that the first and principal acts of government openly and avowedly prevented, through forcible interference, the natural results of all trials of physical strength. These much-talked-of laws of nature are violated every time the highway robber is arrested and sent to jail.

Primitive government, when only brute force was employed, was strong enough to secure the just and equitable distribution of wealth. Today, when mental force is everything, and physical force is nothing, it is powerless to accomplish this. This alone proves that government needs to be strengthened in its primary quality—the protection of society. There is no reasoning that applies to one kind of protection that does not apply equally to the other. It is utterly illogical to say that aggrandizement by physical force should be forbidden while aggrandizement by mental force or legal fiction should be permitted. It is absurd to claim that injustice committed by muscle should be regulated, while that committed by brain be unrestrained.

While the modern plutocracy is not a form of government in the same sense that the other forms mentioned are, it is, nevertheless, easy to see that its power is as great as any government has ever wielded. The test of governmental power is usually the manner in which it taxes the people, and the strongest indictments ever drawn up against the worst forms of tyranny have been those which recited their oppressive methods of extorting tribute. But tithes are regarded as oppressive, and a fourth part of the yield of any industry would justify a revolt. Yet today there are many commodities for which the people pay two and three times as much as would cover the cost of production, transportation, and exchange at fair wages and fair profits. The monopolies in many lines actually tax the consumer from 25 to 75 percent of the real value of the goods. Imagine an excise tax that should approach these figures! Under the operation of either monopoly or aggressive competition the price of everything is pushed up to the maximum limit that will be paid for the commodity in profitable quantities, and this wholly irrespective of the cost of production. No government in the world has now, or ever had, the power to enforce such an extortion as this. It is a governing power in the interest of favored individuals, which exceeds that of the most powerful monarch or despot that ever wielded a scepter.

What then is the remedy? How can society escape this last conquest of power by the egoistic intellect? It has overthrown the rule of brute force by the establishment of government. It has supplanted autocracy by aristocracy and this by democracy, and now it finds itself in the coils of plutocracy. Can it escape? Must it go back to autocracy for a power sufficient to cope with plutocracy? No autocrat ever had a tithe of that power. Shall it then let itself be crushed? It need not. There is one form of government that is stronger than autocracy or aristocracy or democracy, or even plutocracy, and that is *sociocracy*.

The individual has reigned long enough. The day has come for society to take its affairs into its own hands and shape its own destinies. The individual has acted as best he could. He has acted in the only way he could. With a consciousness, will, and intellect of his own he could do nothing else than pursue his natural ends. He should not be denounced nor called any names. He should not even be blamed. Nay, he should be praised, and even *imitated*. Society should learn its great lesson from him, should follow the path he has so clearly laid out that leads to success. It should imagine itself an individual, with all the interests of an individual, and becoming fully *conscious* of these interests it should pursue them with the same indomitable *will* with which the individual pursues his interests. Not only this, it must be guided, as he is guided, by the social *intellect*, armed with all the knowledge that all individuals combined, with so great labor, zeal, and talent have placed in its possession, constituting the social intelligence.

Sociocracy will differ from all other forms of government that have been devised, and yet that difference will not be so radical as to require a revolution. Just as absolute monarchy passed imperceptibly into limited monarchy, with this, in many states without even a change of name has passed into more or less pure democracy, which is now known. For, through paradoxical democracy, which is now the weakest of all forms of government, at least in the control of its own internal elements, is capable of becoming the strongest. Indeed, none of the other forms of government would be capable of passing directly into a government by society. Democracy is a phase through which they must first pass on any route that leads to the ultimate social stage which all governments must eventually attain if they persist.

How then, it may be asked, do democracy and sociocracy differ? How does society differ from the people? If the phrase "the people" really meant the people, the difference would be less. But the shibboleth of democratic states, where it means anything at all that can be described or defined, stands simply for the majority of qualified electors, no matter how small that majority may be. There is a sense in which the action of a majority may be looked upon as the action of society. At least, there is no denying the right of the majority to act for society, for to do this would involve either the denial of the right of government to act at all, or the admission of the right of a minority to act for society. But a majority acting for a society is a different thing from society acting for itself, even though, as must always be the case, it acts through an agency chosen by its members. All democratic governments are largely party governments. The electors range themselves on one side or the other of some party line, the winning side considers itself the state as much as Louis the XIV did. The losing party usually then regards the government as something alien to it and hostile, like an invader, and thinks of nothing but to gain strength enough to overthrow it at the next opportunity. While various issues are always brought forward and defended or attacked, it is obvious to the looker-on that the contestants care nothing for these, and merely use them to gain an advantage and win an election.

From the standpoint of society this is child's play. A very slight awakening of the social consciousness will banish it and substitute something more business-like. Once [we] get rid of this puerile gaming spirit and have attention drawn to the real interests of society, and it will be seen that upon nearly all important questions all parties and all citizens are agreed, and that there is no need of this partisan strain upon the public energies. This is clearly shown at every change in the party complexion of the government. The victorious party which has been denouncing the government merely because it was in the hands of its political opponents boasts that it is going to revolutionize the country in the interest of good government, but the moment it comes into power and feels the weight of national responsibility it finds that it has little to do but carry out the laws in the same way that its predecessors had been doing.

There is a vast difference between all this outward show of partisanship and advocacy of so-called principles, and attention to the real interests and necessary business of the nation, which latter is what the government must do. It is a social duty. The pressure which is brought to enforce it is the power of the social will. But in the factitious excitement of partisan struggles where professional politicians and demagogues on the one hand, and the agents of plutocracy on the other, are shouting discordantly in the ears of people, the real interests of society are, temporarily at least, lost sight of, clouded and obscured, and men lose their grasp on the real issues, forget even their own best interest, which, however selfish, would be a far safer guide, and the general result usually is that these are neglected and nations continue in the hands of mere politicians who are easily managed by the shrewd representatives of wealth.

Sociocracy will change all this. Irrelevant issues will be laid aside. The important objects upon which all but an interested few are agreed will receive their proper degree of attention, and measures will be considered in a non-partisan spirit with the sole purpose of securing these objects. Take as an illustration the postal telegraph question. No one not a stockholder in an existing telegraph company would prefer to pay twenty-five cents for a message if he could sent it for ten cents. Where is the room for discussing a question of this nature? What society wants is the cheapest possible system. It wants to know with certainty whether a national postal telegraph system would secure this universally desired object. It is to be expected that the agents of the present telegraph companies would try to show that it would not succeed. ... But why be influenced by the interests of such a small number of persons, however worthy, when all the rest of mankind are interested in the opposite solution? The investigation should be a disinterested and strictly scientific one, and should actually settle the question in one way or the other. If it was found to be a real benefit, the system should be adopted. There are today a great number of these strictly social questions before the American people, questions which concern every citizen in the country, and whose solution would doubtless profoundly affect the state of civilization attainable on this continent. Not only is it impossible to secure this, but it is impossible to secure an investigation of them on their real merits. The same is true of other countries, and in general the prevailing democracies of the world are incompetent to deal with problems of social welfare.

The prices of most of the staple commodities consumed by mankind have no necessary relation to the cost of producing them and placing them in the hands of the consumer. It is always the highest price that the consumer will pay rather than do without. Let us suppose that price to be on an average double what it would cost to produce, transport, exchange, and deliver the goods, allowing in each of these transactions a fair compensation for all services rendered. Is there any member of society who would prefer to pay two dollars for what is fairly worth only one? Is there any sane ground for arguing such a question? Certainly not. The individual cannot correct this state of things. No democracy can correct it. But a government that really represented the interests of society would no more tolerate it than an individual would tolerate a continual extortion of money on the part of another without an equivalent.

And so it would be throughout. Society would inquire in a business way without fear, favor, or bias, into everything that concerned its welfare, and if it found obstacles it would remove them, and if it found opportunities it would improve them. In a word, society would do under the same circumstances just what an intelligent individual would do. It would further, in all possible ways, its own interests.

I anticipate the objection that this is an ideal state of things, and that it has never been attained by any people, and to all appearances never can be. No fair-minded critic will, however, add the customary objection that is raised, not wholly without truth, to all socialistic schemes, that they presuppose a change in "human nature." Because in the transformation here foreshadowed the permanence of all the mental attributes is postulated, and I have not only refrained from dwelling upon the moral progress of the world, but have not even enumerated among the social forces the power of sympathy as a factor in civilization. I recognize this factor as one of the derivative ones, destined to perform an important part, but I have preferred to rest the case upon the primary and original egoistic influences, believing that neither meliorism nor sociocracy is dependent upon any sentiment, or upon altruistic props for support. At least the proofs will be stronger if none of these aids are called in, and if they can be shown to have a legitimate influence, this is only so much added to the weight of evidence.

To the other charge the answer is that ideals are necessary, and also that no ideal is ever fully realized. If it can be shown that society is actually moving toward any ideal the ultimate substantial realization of that ideal is as good as proved. The proofs of such a movement in society today are abundant. In many countries the encroachments of egoistic individualism have been checked at a number of important points. In this country alarm has been taken in good earnest at the march of plutocracy under the protection of democracy. Party lines are giving way and there are unmistakable indications that a large proportion of the people are becoming seriously interested in social progress of the country. For the first time in the history of political parties there has been formed a distinctively industrial party which possesses all the elements of permanence and may soon be a controlling factor in American politics. Though this may not as yet presage a great social revolution, still it is precisely the way in which a reform in the direction indicated should be expected to originate. But whether the present movement prove enduring or ephemeral, the seeds of reform have been sown broadcast throughout the land, and sooner or later they must spring up, grow, and bear their fruit.

For a long time to come social action must be chiefly negative and be confined to the removal of evils that exist, but a positive stage will ultimately be reached in which society will consider and adopt measures for its own advancement. The question of the respective provinces of social action and individual action cannot be entered into here at length, but it is certain that the former will continue to encroach upon the latter so long as such encroachment is a public benefit. There is one large field in which there is no question on this point, viz., the field covered by what, in modern economic parlance, is called "natural monopoly." The arguments are too familiar to demand restatement here, and the movement is already so well under way that there is little need of further argument. As to what lies beyond this, however, there is room for much discussion and honest difference of opinion. This is because there has been so little induction. It is the special characteristic of the form of government that I have called sociocracy, resting as it does directly upon the science of sociology, to investigate the facts bearing on every subject, not for the purpose of depriving any class of citizens of the opportunity to benefit themselves, but purely and solely for the purpose of ascertaining what is for the best interests of society at large.

The socialistic arguments in favor of society taking upon itself the entire industrial operations of the world have never seemed to me conclusive, chiefly because they have consisted so largely of pure theory and *a priori* deductions. Anyone who has become imbued by the pursuit of some special branch of science with the nature of scientific evidence requires the presentation of such evidence before he can accept conclusions in any other department. And this should be the attitude of all in relation to these broader questions of social phenomena. The true economist can scarcely go farther than to say that a given question is an open one, and that he will be ready to accept the logic of facts when these are brought forward. I do not mean that we must not go into the water until we have learned to swim. This, however, suggests the true method of solving such questions. One learns to swim by a series of trials, and society can well afford to try experiments in certain directions and note the results. There are, however, other methods, such as careful estimates of the costs and accurate calculations of the effect based on the uniform laws of social phenomena. Trial is the ultimate test of scientific theory thus formed, and may, in social as in physical science, either establish or overthrow hypotheses. But in social science, no less than in other branches of science, the working hypothesis must always be the chief instrument of successful research.

Until the scientific stage is reached, and as a necessary introduction to it, social problems may properly be clearly stated and such general considerations brought forward as have a direct bearing upon them. I know of no attempts of this nature which I can more warmly recommend than those made by John Stuart Mill in his little work *On Liberty,* and in his *Chapters on Socialism,* of which the latter appeared posthumously. They are in marked contrast, by their all-sided wisdom, with the intensely one-sided writings of Herbert Spencer on substantially the same subject; and yet the two authors are obviously at one on the main points discussed. This candid statement of the true claims of the *laissez-faire* school is perfectly legitimate. Equally so are like candid presentations of the opposite side of the question. The more light that can be shed on all sides the better, but in order really to elucidate social problems it must be the dry light of science, as little influenced by feeling as though it were the inhabitants of Jupiter's moons, instead of those of this planet, that were under the field of the intellectual telescope.

Appendix B

SOCIOCRACY
Democracy as It Might Be

Kees Boeke (1884-1966)

⟪✳⟫

*Kees Boeke was an internationally known peace activist and edu-
cator. During WW II when he was arrested for harboring Jews, in
his pocket was found a declaration entitled "No Dictatorship" that
nearly cost him his life. This manuscript was an early draft of a plan
for a truly democratic society that was first published in May of 1945
under this title. The following article is from a subsequent version
edited by his wife Beatrice Cadbury Boeke and printed with the permission of his daughter Candia Boeke.*

We are so accustomed to majority rule as a necessary part of
democracy that it is difficult to imagine any democratic system working without it. It is true that it is better to count heads than to break
them, and democracy, even as it is today, has much to recommend it
as compared with former practices. But the party system has proved
very far from providing the ideal democracy of people's dreams. Its
weaknesses have become clear enough: endless debates in Parliament,
mass meetings in which the most primitive passions are aroused, the
overruling by the majority of all independent views, capricious and
unreliable election results, government action rendered inefficient by
the minority's persistent opposition. Strange abuses also creep in. Not
only can a party obtain votes by deplorably underhanded methods,
but, as we all know, a dictator can win an election with an "astonish-
ing" majority by intimidation.

The fact is that we have taken the present system for granted for so long that many people do not realize that the party system and majority rule are not an essential part of democracy. If we really wish to see the whole population united, like a big family, in which the members care for each other's welfare as much as for their own, we must set aside the quantitative principle of the right of the greatest number and find another way of organizing ourselves. This solution must be really democratic in the sense that it must enable each one of us to share in organizing the community. But this kind of democracy will not depend on power, not even the power of the majority. It will have to be a real community-democracy, an organization of the community by the community itself.

For this concept I shall use the word "sociocracy." Such a concept would be of little value if it had never been tried out in practice. But its validity has been successfully demonstrated over the years. Anyone who knows England or America will have heard of the Quakers, the Society of Friends. They have had much influence in these countries and are well known for their practical social work. For more than three hundred years the Quakers have used a method of self-government that rejects majority voting, group action being possible only when unanimity has been reached. I too have found by trying out this method in my school that it really does work, provided there is recognition that the interests of others are as real and as important as one's own. If we start with this fundamental idea, a spirit of goodwill is engendered which can bind together people from all levels of society and with the most varied points of view. This, my school, with its three to four hundred members, has clearly shown.

As a result of these two experiences, I have come to believe that it should be possible some day for people to govern themselves in this way in a much wider field. Many will be highly skeptical about this possibility. They are so accustomed to a social order in which decisions are made by the majority or by a single person, that they do not realize that, if a group provides its own leadership and everyone knows that only when common agreement is reached can any action be taken, quite a different atmosphere is created from that arising from majority rule. These are two examples of sociocracy in practice; let us hope that its principles may be applied on a national, and finally an international scale.

Before describing how the system could be made to work, we must first see what the problem really is. We want a group of persons to establish a common arrangement of their affairs which all will respect and obey. There will be no executive committee chosen by the majority, having the power to command the individual. The group itself must reach a decision and enter into an agreement on the understanding that every individual in the group will act on this decision and honor this agreement. I have called this the self-discipline of the group. It can be compared to the self-discipline of the individual who has learned to set certain demands for himself that he obeys.

There are three fundamental rules underlying the system. The first is that the interests of all members must be considered, the individual bowing to the interests of the whole. Secondly, solutions must be sought which everyone can accept: otherwise no action can be taken. Thirdly, all members must be ready to act according to these decisions when unanimously made.

The spirit that underlies the first rule is really nothing else but concern for one's neighbor, and where this exists, where there is sympathy for other people's interests, where love is, there will be a spirit in which real harmony is possible.

The second point must be considered in more detail. If a group in any particular instance is unable to decide upon a plan of action acceptable to every member, it is condemned to inactivity; it can do nothing. This may happen even today where the majority is so small that efficient action is not possible. But in the case of sociocracy there is a way out, since such a situation stimulates its members to seek for a solution, that everyone can accept, perhaps ending in a new proposal, which had not occurred to anyone before. While under the party system disagreement accentuates the differences and the division becomes sharper than ever, under a sociocratic system, so long as it is realized that *agreement* must be reached, it activates a common search that brings the whole group nearer together. Something must be added here. If no agreement is possible, this usually means that the present situation must continue for the time being. It might seem that in this way conservatism and reaction would reign, and no progress would be possible. But experience has shown that the contrary is true. The mutual trust that is accepted as the basis of a sociocratic society leads inevitably to progress, and this is noticeably greater when all go forward together with something everyone has agreed to. Again it is

clear that there will have to be "higher-level" meetings of chosen representatives, and if a group is to be represented in such a meeting, it
will have to be by someone in whom everyone has confidence. If this
does not prove possible, then the group will not be represented at all
in the higher-level meeting, and its interests will have to be cared for
by the representatives of other groups. But experience has shown that
where representation is not a question of power but of trust, the choice
of a suitable person can be made fairly easily and without unpleasantness.

The third principle means that when agreement is reached the
decision is binding on all who have made it. This also holds of the
higher-level meeting for all who have sent representatives to it. There
is a danger in the fact that each must keep decisions made in a meeting
over which he has only an indirect influence. This danger is common
to all such decisions, not least in the party system. But it is much less
dangerous where the representatives are chosen by common consent
and are therefore much more likely to be trusted.

A group that works in this way should be of particular size. It
must be big enough for personal matters to give way to an objective
approach to the subject under discussion, but small enough not to be
unwieldy, so that the quiet atmosphere needed can be secured. For
meetings concerned with general aims and methods a group of about
forty has been found the most suitable. But when detailed decisions
have to be made, a small committee will be needed of three to six persons or so. This kind of committee is not new. If we could have a look
at the countless committees in existence, we should probably find that
those that are doing the best work do so without voting. They decide
on a basis of common consent. If a vote were to be taken in such a
small group, it would usually mean that the atmosphere is wrong.

Of special importance in exercising sociocratic government is
the leadership. Without a proper leader unanimity cannot easily be
reached. This concerns a certain technique that has to be learnt. Here
Quaker experience is of the greatest value. Let me describe a Quaker
business meeting. The group comes together in silence. In front sits
the Clerk, the leader of the meeting. Beside him sits the Assistant
Clerk; who writes down what is agreed upon. The Clerk reads out each
subject in turn, after which all members present, men and women, old
and young, may speak to the subject. They address themselves to the

meeting and not to a chairman, each one making a contribution to the developing train of thought. It is the Clerk's duty, when he thinks the right moment has come, to read aloud a draft minute reflecting the feeling of the meeting. It is a difficult job, and it needs much experience and tact to formulate the sense of the meeting in a way that is acceptable to all. It often happens that the Clerk feels the need for a time of quiet. Then the whole gathering will remain silent for a while, and often out of the silence will come a new thought, a reconciling solution, acceptable to everyone. It may seem unbelievable to many that a meeting of up to a thousand people can be held in this way. And yet I have been present at a Yearly Meeting of the Quakers in London, held during war-time (the First World War), at which the much vexed problem of the Quaker attitude to war was discussed in such a manner, no vote being taken. So I believe that if we once set ourselves the task of learning this method of co-operation, beginning with very simple matters, we shall be able to learn this art and acquire a tradition that will make possible the handling of more difficult questions.

This has been confirmed by my experience at Bilthoven in building up the school which I called the Children's Community Workshop. Very early on I suggested that we should talk over how we should organize our community life. At first the children objected, saying they wanted me to take the decisions for them. But I insisted, and the idea of the 'Talkover," or weekly meeting, was accepted. Later I suggested that one of the children help me with the leadership of the meeting; and from that time on it has become an institution, led by the children, which we should not like to lose.

When I began to hold these Talkovers, I was aware that I was using the procedure of the Quaker business meeting, and I saw in the distance, as it were, the great problem of the government of humanity. It was also curious to discover whether the art of living together, understood as obeying the rule we had all agreed upon, would be simple enough to be learned by children. An experience of some 20 years has shown me that it certainly is.

But something more is necessary before this method can be applied to adult society. When we are concerned, not with a group of a few hundred people, but with thousands, even millions, whose lives we wish to organize in this way, we must accept the principle of some sort of representation. There will have to be higher–level meetings, and these will have to deal with matters concerning a wider area. Higher-level meetings will also have to send representatives to another higher body, which will be responsible for a still wider area, and so on.

After my hopes for the success of school meetings had been confirmed by practice, I was very curious to know if a meeting of representatives would work also in the school. One day when the number of children had grown too large for one general meeting at which all could be present, I suggested the setting up of a meeting of representatives. At first the children did not like the idea; children are conservative. But, as often happens, six months later they suggested the same plan themselves, and since then this institution has become a regular part of the life of the school.

Of course such meetings, if ever they are to be used by adults for the organization of society as a whole, will have a very different character from those of our children's community. But how in practice could such methods be introduced? First of all, a Neighborhood Meeting, made up of perhaps forty families, might be set up in a particular district, uniting those who live near enough to one another, so that they could easily meet. In a town it very often happens that people do not even know their neighbors, and it will be an advantage if they are forced to take an interest in those who live close by. The Neighborhood Meeting might embrace about 150 people, including children. About 40 of these Neighborhood Meetings might send representatives to a Ward Meeting, acting for something like 6000 people. In general it will be true to say that the wider the area the Meeting governs the less often it will need to meet. The representatives of about 40 Ward Meetings could come together in a District Meeting, acting for about 240,000 people.

In approximately 40 or 50 District Meetings the whole population of a small country might be covered. The representatives would bring the interests of all the Districts to a Central Meeting. It is an essential condition that representatives have the confidence of the whole group: if they have that, business can usually be carried on quickly and effectively.

As the whole sociocratic method depends on trust, there will be no disadvantage if, alongside the geographical representation of Neighborhood, Ward, District and Central Meetings, a second set of functional groupings be established. It seems reasonable that all industries and professions send representatives to primary, secondary and, where necessary, tertiary meetings, and that the trusted representatives of the "workers" in every field should be available to give their professional advice to the government. I have here used the word "government". It is not my intention to put forward a plan according to which the government itself could one day be formed on sociocratic lines. We must start from the present situation, and the only possibility is that, with the government's consent, we make a beginning of the sociocratic method from the bottom upwards; that is, for the present, with the formation of Neighborhood groups. We, ordinary people, must just learn to talk over our common interests and to reach agreement after quiet consideration, and this can be done best in the place where we live. Only after we have seen how difficult this is, and after, most probably, making many mistakes, will it be possible to set up meetings on a higher level. If leaders should emerge in the Neighborhood Meetings, their advice would gradually be seen to be useful in the existing Local Councils. Later, in the same way, the advice of leaders of Ward Meetings would be of increasing value.

The sociocratic method must recommend itself by the efficiency with which it works. When the governing power has learnt to trust it enough so as to allow, perhaps even to encourage, the setting up of Neighborhood Meetings, the system will be able to show what possibilities it has, and then the confidence of the governing bodies and of people at large will have a chance to grow. I can well believe that trusted leaders and representatives of Neighborhood Meetings may be allowed, or even invited, to attend Local Meetings. These men and women will of course take no part in the voting, for sociocracy does not believe in voting; but they might be allowed a place in the centre between the "left" and the "right". After a time it may even be deemed desirable to ask them for advice about the matter in hand, since it would previously have been discussed in their Neighborhood Meetings, and a solution sought acceptable to all. It is conceivable that, as confidence grows, certain matters might be handed over to the Neighborhood Meetings with the necessary funds to carry them out. Only when the value of the new system is realized, could the higher-level meetings be begun.

Is such a development as this a fantasy? When we consider the possible success of government on the sociocratic principle, one thing is certain; it is unthinkable unless it is accompanied and supported by the conscious education of old and young in the sociocratic method. The right kind of education is essential, and here a revolution is needed in our schools. Only latterly have attempts been made in them to further the spontaneous development of the child and encourage his initiative. Partly because the stated aim of the school is to impart knowledge and skills, and partly because people regard obedience as a virtue in itself, children have been trained to obey. We are only beginning to realize the dangers of this practice. If children are not taught to judge for themselves, they will in later life become an easy prey for the dictator. But if we really want to prepare youth to think and act for themselves, we must alter our attitude to education. The children should not be sitting passively in rows, while the schoolmaster drills a lesson into their heads. They should be able to develop freely in children's communities, guided and helped by those who are older acting as their comrades. Initiative should be fostered in every possible way. They should learn from the beginning to do things for themselves, and to make things necessary in their school life. But above all they should learn how to run their own community in some such way as has already been described.

Finally we must return to the question of representation. We have not gone further than the government of our own country. But the great problem of the government of mankind can never be solved on a national basis. Every country is dependent for raw materials and products on other countries. It is therefore inevitable that the system of representation should be extended over a whole continent and representatives of continents join in a World Meeting to govern and order the whole world. Our technical skill in the fields of transport and organization make something of this kind possible. Finally a World Meeting should invite representatives of all the continents to arrange a reasonable distribution of all raw materials and products, making them available for all mankind. So long as we are ruled by fear and distrust, it is impossible to solve the problems of the world. The more trust grows and the more fear diminishes, the more the problem will shrink.

Everything depends on a new spirit breaking through among men. May it be that, after the many centuries of fear, suspicion and hate, more and more a spirit of reconciliation and mutual trust will spread abroad. The constant practice of the art of sociocracy and of the education necessary for it seem to be the best way in which to further this spirit, upon which the real solution of all world problems depends.

Rationale for a New Social Design
Gerard Endenburg (1933–)

⟨❦⟩

Gerard Endenburg, a former student of Kees Boeke and a graduate of the Children's Community Workshop, developed the first widely used principles and methods of sociocracy. Beginning with the principles that Kees Boeke developed, Endenburg incorporated what he had learned from cybernetics and systems thinking to structuring and governing all organizations. In this selection from Sociocracy as Social Design, *first published in Dutch in 1995 and in English in 1998, Endenburg talks in this passage about how he developed sociocracy in his company, Endenburg Electrotechniek. (Edited with some re-translation by the authors.)*

At the end of the nineteen-sixties, I began to look for another way of running a business. With the inequality of individuals in the exercise of power or the making of decisions, traditional organizations with their authoritarian leadership were then seen by many, including myself, to be one of the most important causes of violence. By *violence* I mean that by which another, I or *the* other, can be denied or ignored.

From the standpoint of equality, I also distrusted the democratic way of making decisions—the principle of majority rule. The question was, "What should a business look like to avoid this inequality?"

For this reason, whenever anyone developed a new form of organization, I wanted to test it in practice. As a result, a fruitful exchange began between development and application. Having one's own company offered a unique opportunity to do this.

In my view, however, all the experiments with other forms of organization of which I was aware were ultimately authoritarian, or democratic, in character. These included organizations built on a cooperative basis, companies with workers' self-government as in the former Yugoslavia, the Mondragon project in Spain, the Scott Bader Company and the Glacier Project in England, van Steenis in the Netherlands, and many others. Inequivalence of value was always embedded in the decision-making process in these organizations. Consequently, evaluating these experiments only made sense to me if the manner of decision-making prevailing in the organization was neither autocratic nor democratic. Although at that time I much preferred the democratic method of decision making to the autocratic method, as a result of my own experience I later came to distrust democracy even more. It was not only majority rule that provoked my resistance; there was far more to distrust. My schooling under Kees Boeke served me well here. In fact, my experience of education based on Quaker principles was enormously important.

Both I and Others

United in the Religious Society of Friends, Quakers experience their religion each in their own personal way. This involves firstly a fundamental respect for the religious experience and the religious reality of others. The equivalence of each individual derives from this principle. Furthermore, they have never fixed their religion in images, they have no church, and there are no priests. Whenever they come together, silence is the source of their inspiration. Decision making is by general consensus and non-violence is one of their basic principles. Kees Boeke, for whom these Quaker principles had a universal validity, based his school, De Werkplaats Kindergemeenschap (The Children's Community Workshop), on them, and as a consequence I had already had in my youth some experience of the "both-and" concept. The test in practice was to see whether one's own interests could be served by serving the interests of the other, in this case both I and the other(s) with whom I worked. I also learned to decide by general consensus to have respect for the ideas of others and to build with the group of which I was a part both my own and my collective world, or reality.

In the group of which I was a part and in other groups at the school, nothing was ever decided by the majority. When majority rule was once tried, the feeling of the group was so altered that we rapidly abandoned it. It seemed as though something violent had happened.

Initially, these experiences formed the only—but essential—data on which my distrust of democracy was based.

Lack of Knowledge about Control of Power

I found it enormously irritating that no one could provide any theoretical support for any form of decision making whatever. Why was democracy the principle on which our whole way of life was based?

I began to form the idea that a great deal of what we experience as problems of power had their root in a lack of knowledge, whether partial or complete, about the control of power or, more specifically, about the control of dynamic processes. It appeared as though nothing from the technical sciences, the area of my own expertise, had managed to penetrate either the social sciences or the practice of organization and control. This was, for me, the point of departure for the process of developing sociocracy.

The various forms of control based on decisively cutting through problems, with which we have become so familiar, are all the result of ignoring the possibilities of integrated control based on circular processes. What all these variations have in common is that an institution of supremacy is created (i.e., a chairperson, major shareholder, representative group, or organ) and allotted a dominant position without this dominance or supremacy itself being in any way open to creation or re-creation using a circular process. If so, it would be self-governing through a mutual exchange of arguments. Indeed, argument and the exchange of arguments in such an institution do not openly cycle but rather they occur within the process of acquiring and assuming the position of dominance, functioning only to rationalize and legitimize that process. They exist within the framework of a competitive struggle for supremacy to which they are then bound in servitude.

Here, I use the term *power* in the sense of the ability to influence. (Everything that is, that exists, is a manifestation of power.) Viewed in this way, all the factors capable of influencing our lives are factors of power. Influence is a universal phenomenon that accompanies the actualization of power.

Supremacy is an absolute or authoritarian variant of this power. Supremacy arises where influence can be monopolized or power actualized from an isolated position. Supremacy thus represents the possibility of violence: the ability to deny others and the other.

Delegation of Power to the *"Argument"*

The idea of "sociocracy succeeding democracy" began to emerge. At the end of the nineteen-sixties, I spoke of the triad—autocracy, democracy, and sociocracy—as methods in an evolutionary sequence to shape and direct our lives and living together. In theory, according to this sequence, in the method of autocracy, a supremacy is granted to an individual or a small select group; in the democratic method, to the majority; and in the sociocratic method, to the *argument*. What this means is an argument in which the *I* and the *other* are so connected that there are no apparent grounds to either party for denying consent in order to achieve supremacy. Shifting supremacy to the principle of "argument" has practical consequences for it precisely precludes the exclusion of the other person and the other from possible influence and contribution. Sociocracy can thus be seen as a social design whose aim is to offer no opportunity for the appropriation or consolidation of supremacy. Because of this, the sociocratic method corresponds more closely and explicitly with the scientific method than is the case with democratic governance. What is proposed here, as a modification of Feyerabend's famous dictum against scientific method (Feyerabend 1975) to become "Anything goes under the understanding that any thing goes."

Under the principle of consent (the principle of no objection), as I understand it, a decision is only made when no one involved has any strong and argued objection. This is where individual equivalence is determined. By embracing everyone's argument, discussion gives everyone concerned the chance to reach the best solution, one that is practicable for all.

A paramount and argued objection is one that:

- is indisputable by reason of its grounds for withholding consent

- demonstrates a reason or motive that has been ignored or underestimated by those attending and/or the statement presented

- takes the form of a rejection of the proposal because the reason or motive has not been adequately considered in the decision proposed.

Once reasoned consent predominates it governs the process of decision making, subordinating all other ways of reaching a decision, i.e. they are only possible if consent exists for them.

Guiding of Power Following the Principles of Cybernetics

Literally, *sociocracy* means the sovereignty of the *socius*: I myself, the next person, the alter ego, the otherness. From a structural point of view this corresponds with the definition of sociocracy as a situation where the principle of consent predominates or is socially all–determining in the sense that it governs the making of decisions at all levels of society. The sociocratic circle organization is a cybernetic means of making this possible and then, as a dynamic balance, it maintains, regulates, and develops it.

With sociocratic circle organization there arises the possibility, in fact, to guide power according to cybernetic principles. Sociocracy is in this way also a method, an organizing, a possible ongoing process of construction, reconstruction, and deconstruction. It is a method that in itself is "empty," since every view, ideology, conviction, or method, etc., that might be attached can find its place and influence in it. Only that which serves absolutely to isolate is excluded. Sociocracy is based on the idea that there is no given or permanent base to which social reality can be secured. What is produced as group organization contains an "objective" reality construct: it gives the possibilities that can be inter-subjectively explored. It provides a new basis for our society that will replace the democratic, which in its own turn replaced the autocratic. At the time, I therefore called this, the sociocratic circle organization, a basis for living and working together.

With regard to the concept of supremacy, the "one man–one vote" system represents an equality that gives to democracy the appearance of individual equivalence. For the minority, however, the majority means simply a supremacy, a respectable and established means of voting away the interests of the minority. My distrust of democracy only deepened as the sociocratic design developed. The sociocratic way of dealing with power through organizing comprises self-organization in continual relation with that which links that organizing self with the other, the outer world. In this way, sociocracy goes beyond the fixations, the sectarian divisions and limitations that the democratic way of handling power demonstrably amplifies.

In the early nineteen-seventies, I began to apply this design-in-embryo, as a circular process, to the organization of my company. From then on, the process of continuous construction, reconstruction, and deconstruction of the organization became part of the normal routine. Decision-making, investing, ownership—everything was part of the discussion. Every proposal, every argument during the circle meetings had equal value in decision making. Everything that belonged in the circle could be discussed, nothing was excluded, not even salaries or personal matters. The way of electing people, after open discussion with consent, was a part of this.

In the beginning of 1976, the shipbuilding industry collapsed, leading to a crisis that had near catastrophic consequences for the company. By the end of that critical year, once it became clear that the greatest threat to our further existence was over with hardly any layoffs, not only was there rejoicing at our shared success but some considerable amazement, too, at the way that had been achieved. Was the tenacity and creativity of the circles the strength of the sociocratic circle organization?

It was indisputable that sociocracy had contributed to this success, though that contribution is of course difficult to quantify or to demonstrate objectively. The consequence was in any case an unexpected development of the design and, as a result, the sociocratic circle organization acquired a wider significance. Ever since, the possibility of generating, regenerating, degenerating, and repairing starting from chaos has had a recognizable place and function in the sociocratic circle. During this process, which had been generated and sociocratically regulated as result of the crisis, it was discovered that it was vitally important for an organization not only to allow room and influence for the methods of making decisions that is so distinctive of sociocracy, democracy, and autocracy, but also to the decision making methods characteristic of religion and chaos.

The following suggest themselves as principles for methods of decision making that characterize respectively these ways of thinking:

Sociocracy: The principle of consent. Supremacy belongs to the arguments that the individual and the community (with possible inclusion of "the outside world") present to one another.

Democracy: The principle of the majority. Supremacy is given to the greatest number, the most inclusive representation, the most shares, etc.

Autocracy: The principle of the individual or a small, select group. Supreme power given to the Leader, the Superior, the owner, the aristocratic caste, or the expert.

Theocracy: The principle of a totally binding belief or unity. Supreme power is delegated to the "it," the all-inclusive crystallization point in yourself, the other person, and also in *the* other.

Chaos: Emergence from possibilities that are not immediately coherent. Supremacy given to incoherent power phenomenon or possibilities of presence.

A Place for Chaos

Starting from chaos, i.e. from a system of possibilities without interconnections understood between them, new ideas are born, problems solved, and the pioneering starts. An organization must literally make room for this. A place for chaos, where there needs to be no connections and where existing connections must be undone and new forms thought up. With sociocracy, that place is the circle meeting, the place where continuous construction, reconstruction, and deconstruction of the work of the organization can occur, where the events and episodes themselves can be looked at and where experiences (intuitions and feelings) can be exchanged. *The circle organization should, in this regard, be seen as an infrastructure for reflection. Decision making in the circle is governed by the principle of consent. Through reflection the application of the principle of consent becomes a process of self-investigation and self-renewal. As a result, the continuance of equivalence in decision-making is possible for those involved. It becomes a reflexive principle of consent.*

Application of the principle of consent on its own, without being organically integrated in a circle structure, is not advised since there is then no provision for reflection, leading to a kind of "equivalence in no-man's land" which could be eventually applied as a means of manipulation. As will be further explained in the course of the fol-

lowing chapter, no real human equivalence is possible without organic integration in a circle structure.

During the circle meeting all possible structural changes and policy proposals are discussed, without there being any necessity to alter the existing structure. After deciding by consent in such a "brainstorming" session on new possibilities, the changes can be carried through. These new possibilities must always link up functionally with the circle members and their collective objective. It can also be proposed that circle members themselves should take a prominent part in expanding the repertoire of new prospects. In the "brainstorming" stage of the circle meeting, their mutual relations and connections that are determined and operative in the workplace can be loosened. The result is to create a forum of chaos and synergy, where each member of the circle can display his or her possibilities, in order to be able to push further, as much for their own benefit as for the benefit of other circle members. It is a forum in which everyone can freely move without risk of being put down. On the strength of consent alone, structural changes can be developed at the decision-making stage.

Because the circle meeting is preeminently a breeding place for an organization, a business for example, where generation, regeneration, and degeneration can occur, it is by no means an optional luxury but vitally important for organizing. Within a company, the organization of work that is provided with a sociocratic circle organization, shows a capacity to construct, reconstruct, and deconstruct, strongly enhancing continuity. In actual fact, it is the people in a sociocratic circle organization who determine this continuity. The possibility of eternal life? In any case, in principle and excluding unforeseen calamities, there is the possibility of keeping the organization functioning as long as needed.

After chaos, religion. Once a decision is made, with the binding unity formed by consent, the circle can believe in that decision— and necessarily so, for otherwise nothing will succeed. The same is true for those functions and tasks that are delegated to individuals by consent. Cooperation is impossible unless one can believe in this delegation, the embodiment of unity through diversification.

There is then a need for space for independent decision making (which is authoritarian in the sense that the individual derives the power to dominate through consent) in order to be able to fulfill the functions and tasks delegated. All forms of decision-making can thus be successfully implemented provided they are governed by the principle of consent. Within the governing structure that consent decision-making provides, it turns out in practice that there is hardly any use for the democratic way of making decisions—another signal that only confirmed my doubts over the capacity for resolution of the democratic method.

A Self-Controlling Process

Thus the sociocratic circle organization as a basis for living and working together not only rests on decision making according to the principle of consent but also allows the possibility for chaos, religion, autocracy, and democracy to exist within it. These possibilities present themselves one after the other, but in actual practice, when organizing decision making, they present themselves at the same time, in what are called *parallel processes.*

The development which accompanies this broadening of the basis also makes it clear that simply laying a basis is not sufficient. More is needed if the process is to be capable of further self-development and of self-direction. *Basis* here means the starting point from which the process of construction, reconstruction, and deconstruction can take place in a reasonably dignified way. The question remained, however: how can organizing be produced and directed so that equivalence remains integrally present within it, and such that the reciprocal movements of being led and the unfolding of self initiative can maintain a forward momentum?

By the beginning of the nineteen-eighties I was wondering: "Is there anything known about the shaping and direction of organization as process, and if so where can I get instruction?" What had so far come to my notice from various disciplines had not produced much of a satisfactory result. This was around the time that the in-company training systems of many companies were folding because of financial constrictions. I, on the contrary, with my awareness tuned by my education at Boeke's school, was coming to the conclusion that, because of the speed of developments, permanent education was vital to any company and that for this requirement traditional educational establishments could never in the long run be wholly satisfactory. The term "permanent education" here covers three categories of education:

firstly, vocational education in the relevant field; secondly, education in the structuring of the organization as process; and thirdly, education in the organization of decision making. In the traditional approach, vocational education is primarily concerned with the first category, but this is of limited value given the speed of developments taking place in the various specialties. It would probably be better to deliver this kind of education within the company.

The two other subjects, to which far too little attention is still given, probably lend themselves ideally to a regular, formal practical education, since they involve the acquisition of skills and practical know–how that is less context and time dependent.

In my own company, we began shaping and integrating this permanent education in the early eighties, under the name of "integral education." With a good basis alone, only part of the problem was resolved. It was necessary to develop the lacking knowledge and skills as rapidly as possible.

As a result of the enormous energy that I myself put into the development of this matter of structuring and directing at this stage, I arrived at the discovery with which my intuition of the deficiency of democracy could be given a clear foundation. In retrospect, that discovery provided the legitimation for the decision not to democratize my company but to provide a sociocratic basis.

Sociocratic Centers & Consultants

Sociocratisch Centrum Nederland (SCN)

The Sociocratisch Centrum is the primary source of information on sociocracy. It maintains a website in English and Dutch that includes a basic explanation of the sociocratic circle-organization method, its history, information on implementation, Network Circles, Certification, Publications, and contacts.

Sociocratisch Centrum

Prins Pieter Christiaanstraat 61

3066 TB Rotterdam

The Netherlands

Telephone: 31-10-4523289

Email: info@sociocratie.nl

Website: www.sociocratie.nl

Certified Consultants in North America

Governance Alive, LLC

Principal Consultant: John Buck

Governance Alive
1319 Stateside Drive
Silver Spring, MD 20903
USA

Telephone: 1.800.870.2092

Email: contact@governancealive.com

Sociogest

Principal Consultant: Giles Charest

Sociogest
332, Chemin de la Pinerale
Lac Simon, Québec
J0V 1E0

Telephone: 1.819.428.4288
              1.819.428.1560

Website: www.sociogest.ca

Biodynamic Business

Principal Consultant: Tena Meadows O'Rear

Biodynamic Business
12606 Trillium Glen
Lovettsville, VA 20108
USA

Telephone: 540-822-4070

Email: tena.m.orear@gmail.com

For a complete list of individual consultants and facilitators, please see the sociocracy.info website:

www.sociocracy.info/consultants

Other Resources

Sociocracy.info

A comprehensive website of information on sociocracy with a bibliography, links, email discussion groups. etc.

www.sociocracy.info

Appendix E

Operating Agreement & Bylaws
for a Sociocratic Organization

The following example contains the key clauses for a sociocratic operating agreement for a typical Limited Liability Company (LLC) and for bylaws in other kinds of organizations. In the United States, LLCs are now legal in all 50 states and the District of Columbia and currently provide the most efficient mechanism for establishing a fully sociocratic company that owns and governs itself. These clauses specify sociocratic methods for dynamic self-governance of the company and separate ownership from absolute control of the company. While a sociocratic company allows investors and protects the interests of investors, it does not grant them the exclusive right to sell or to govern the company.

With modifications, these clauses can form the basis of bylaws for a nonprofit organization, an association, or a local government agency. They can also be used as the basis of bylaws for a C or S corporation, but in these cases a "double corporation" strategy is required to enable the company to raise capital without giving stockholders the right to override consent decision-making. An explanation of the double corporation is outside the scope of this book but it involves setting up a foundation to hold the controlling stock. The members of the board of the foundation and the board of the corporation are identical.

This operating agreement is an example only and does not constitute legal advice. Because laws differ between jurisdictions, professional legal advice is required to address specific circumstances.

213

Operating Agreement
of a Sociocratic Limited Liability Company (LLC)

ARTICLE 1 THE SOCIOCRATIC (DYNAMIC SELF-GOVERNANCE) METHOD

1.1 Organizational Model

The LLC shall be structured in accordance with the sociocratic (dynamic self-governance) method of organization, the underlying principles of which are as follows:

1.1.1 The Principle of Consent

The principle of consent governs decision-making. This means that not every decision requires consent but that there will be consent about the policies by which decision-making takes a different form. Consent means there are no argued and paramount objections. In other words, a policy decision can only be made if no member of the circle raises a argued and paramount objection to it.

1.1.2 The Principle of Circles

The organization is composed of a hierarchy of semi-autonomous, self-organizing circles. A circle is a group of persons who are operationally related. Each circle has its own aim and has the authority and responsibility to execute, measure, and control its own activities and to maintain an appropriate level of knowledge and skill, assisted by a program of development conducted by the circle.

1.1.3 The Principle of Double-Linked Circles

All circles are double-linked. A lower circle is always linked to a higher circle in such a way that at least two persons, that is, the operational leader and at least one elected representative from the lower circle, belong to and participate in the decision making of the next higher circle.

1.1.4 The Principle of Election of Persons

Persons are elected to functions and tasks exclusively by consent after open discussion.

1.2 Structure

The organization of the LLC shall be a hierarchy of double-linked circles, in the following order, from top to bottom:

1.2.1 Top Circle

The top circle shall be the highest circle of the LLC, the powers and responsibilities of which are set forth in the articles of organization and this operating agreement. The composition of the top circle is defined in Article 2.

The top circle shall manage and direct the business and affairs of the LLC with full power to engage in any lawful act or activity under the General Limited Liability Company (LLC) Law of [name of jurisdiction] unless otherwise limited by the provisions of this operating agreement.

1.2.2 General Circle

The general circle shall consist of the chief executive officer (CEO), operational leaders of the department circles, and at least one representative from each department circle. The general circle shall manage the operations of the LLC within the limits set by the top circle.

The general circle shall:

(a) Determine and control policy to realize its own aim(s) within limits set by the top circle.

(b) Delegate part of its decision-making authority to the department circles so their aims can be achieved.

(c) Assign functions and tasks to its own members to execute its own policy.

(d) Decide, in its sole discretion, whether new department circles should be created or whether existing circles should be split up, combined, or dissolved. The department circle in question may not participate in the decision to dissolve its circle. The consent of the representative of the department circle in question shall not be required for the general circle to act, but such representative may participate in such discussions in the general circle.

1.2.3 Department Circles

Each department circle shall consist of (1) either an operational leader and the members of the department circle or an operational leader and the operational leaders of the section circles and (2) at least one representative from each section circle. The department circle shall:

(a) Determine and control the policy to achieve its aim within the limits set by the general circle.

(b) Assign tasks to its own members to execute its own policy.

(c) Decide, in its sole discretion, whether a new section circle should be set up or whether existing circles should be dissolved. The section circle in question may not participate in the decision to dissolve its circle. The consent of the representative of the section circle in question shall not be required for the department circle to act, but such representative may participate in such discussions in the department circle.

1.2.4 Section Circles

Each section circle shall consist of (1) either an operational leader and the members of the section circle or an operational leader and operational leaders of the unit circles and (2) at least one representative from each unit circle. The section circle shall:

(a) Determine and control policy to achieve their aims within the limits set by the department circle.

(b) Assign tasks to their own members to execute their own policy.

(c) Decide, in its sole discretion, whether new unit circles should be set up or whether existing circles should be dissolved. The unit circle in question may not participate in the decision to dissolve its circle. The consent of the representative of the unit circle in question shall not be required for the section circle to act, but such representative may participate in the discussions in the section circle.

1.2.5 Unit Circles

Each unit circle shall consist of an operational leader and its own members. Unit circles shall:

(a) Determine and control policy to achieve its aim within the limits set by the section circle.

(b) Assign tasks to its own members to execute its own policy.

1.2.6 Further Subdivision

The hierarchical pattern established in sections 1.2.2-1.2.5 shall be repeated for any levels below unit circles.

1.3 Investing and Working Partners

Persons can become members of the LLC by investing money or by performing active labor or both. People or organizations that have made investments in the LLC shall be called hereafter "investing partners." Those who perform labor shall be called hereafter "working partners." Members of the general, department, section, and unit circles, and any circles below unit circles shall be working partners. A natural person can be both a working partner and an investing partner. A legal person, for example, another LLC, S corporation, or C corporation, can be an investing partner but not a working partner.

[The decision to have "working partners" or "employees" has tax and other implications that require legal advice. The intention is that everyone be able to participate in decision making on an equivalent basis. The term "partner" is not intended to infer greater authority nor "employee" less authority.]

ARTICLE 2 TOP CIRCLE

[Top Circle is the generic term for the highest governing level of the organization. It retains the circular process connotations and links to the primary sociocratic theory. Organizations may wish to adopt other terms to reflect their culture and environment.]

2.1 Composition and Number

The top circle shall consist of no less than six (6) nor more than twelve (12) members, as such number may be established from time to time by resolution of the top circle. This number shall include:

(a) external experts,

(b) the CEO of the LLC, and

(c) one or more representatives of the general circle of the LLC.

2.2 External Experts

[The importance of the title "board of directors" varies amongst legal jurisdictions and not all organizations are required to have a board. When a board is required, there may also be a requirement that it be composed entirely of persons from outside the organization, the external experts. If that is the case, the following clause can be used: "The top circle shall totally encompass all the duties of the board of directors. Every meeting of the top circle shall be considered a meeting also of the board of directors. The board of directors shall not meet separately from the top circle." If a board is required by law, it may also be necessary to have a separate article defining the board and its responsibilities. If so, it can be modeled after the clauses used for the top circle.]

The external experts, chosen from outside the organization, shall represent each of the following roles:

(a) A person with expertise in financial matters relating to the business of the LLC.

(b) A person with expertise in the area of human resource management, small business management, or other management specialties.

(c) A person with expertise in sociocratic (dynamic self-governance) or other technical areas in which the LLC may choose to conduct its business.

(d) A representative of the governmental or legal community.

2.3 Separation of Roles

The CEO, elected representatives from the general circle, and the person with expertise in financial matters must be separate persons. These persons and other members of the top circle who are not working partners of the LLC may fulfill one or more than one of the other above roles at the same time unless this could result in a statutory, operational, or legal incompatibility.

2.4 Designation of Roles

The top circle, by resolution, shall designate the roles that each of its members fulfills.

2.5 Election, Terms, and Reimbursement

The members of the top circle, except for the financial expert, may be proposed by an external organization with consent from the CEO and elected representative(s). If such external organizations are not available, the top circle may elect persons with expertise in these areas to participate in the top circle for specified terms. The experts' terms shall be staggered and up to two years in duration, renewable at the invitation of the top circle. The top circle may choose to reimburse these experts for their services.

2.6 Resignation; Vacancies

Any member of the top circle may resign from the top circle at any time by submitting a letter of resignation to the secretary of the top circle

Any newly created membership or any vacancy occurring in the top circle for any cause may be filled by a person selected by the consent of the remaining members of the top circle and each member so elected shall hold office until the expiration of the term of office of the member of the top circle whom he or she has replaced or until his or her successor is elected and qualified.

The CEO shall be elected or re-elected at two-year intervals at the first top circle meeting after the annual investors' meeting. The representative(s) from the general circle shall be elected at intervals of up to two years on a schedule set by the general circle.

2.7 Regular Meetings

Regular meetings of the top circle may be held at such places within or without the [name of jurisdiction] and at such times as the top circle may from time to time determine, and if so determined, notices thereof need not be given.

2.8 Special Meetings

Special meetings of the top circle may be held at any time or place within or without the [name of jurisdiction] whenever called by any member of the top circle. Notice of a special meeting of the top circle shall be given by the person or persons calling the meeting at least forty-eight (48) hours before the special meeting.

2.9 Telephonic Meetings Permitted

Members of the top circle may participate in a meeting thereof by means of conference telephone or similar communications equipment by means of which all persons participating in the meeting can hear each other, and participation in a meeting pursuant to this operating agreement shall constitute presence in person at such meeting.

2.10 Consent Decision Required for Action

The principle of consent by all parties shall be organized as follows: At all meetings of the top circle one-half of the members of the top circle or at least 2 members of the top circle, whichever number is the greater, shall constitute a quorum for the transaction of business. All decision-making by the top circle, however, shall be according to the principle of consent; that is, whether or not a member of the top circle is present, consent is required of all the members of the top circle to all proposed decisions.

Any member of the top circle absent from a meeting of the top circle shall be notified within forty-eight (48) hours of the proposed decision(s) of the top circle. Unless the absent top circle member objects to a decision of the top circle within seventy-two (72) hours of receipt of such notice, he or she will be deemed to have consented to such decision.

If an absent top circle member objects to any action of the top circle in a timely fashion, the matter will be placed upon the agenda for the next meeting of the top circle, which meeting shall be held within seventy-two (72) hours of the receipt of such objection. Any member absent from such top circle meeting shall be deemed to have consented to the decision that the top circle reconsiders.

2.11 Organization

Meetings of the top circle shall be presided over by the president of the top circle or another person chosen by consent of the top circle. In the absence of the president or other chosen person, a chairperson chosen at the meeting shall preside over the meeting. The secretary shall act as secretary of the meeting, but in his or her absence the person presiding may appoint any person to act as secretary of the meeting.

2.12 Informal Actions

Any decision required or permitted to be made at any meeting of the top circle may be made without a meeting if all members of the top circle consent thereto in writing, and the writing or writings are filed with the minutes of proceedings of the top circle.

ARTICLE 3 EXECUTIVE OFFICERS OF THE TOP CIRCLE

3.1 Executive Officers; Election; Qualifications; Term of Office; Resignation; Removal; Vacancies.

The top circle shall annually elect executive officers from amongst its members: a president, secretary, and treasurer and it may, if it so determines, choose a chairperson (or facilitator) of the top circle and a vice chairperson (or second facilitator) of the top circle from among its members. The top circle may also choose one or more vice presidents, one or more assistant vice presidents, one or more assistant secretaries, and one or more assistant treasurers. Each such officer shall hold office until the first meeting of the top circle after the annual meeting of investing partners next succeeding his or her election, and until his or her successor is elected and qualified or until his or her earlier resignation or removal.

Any officer may resign his or her executive office at any time upon written notice to the secretary of the LLC. The secretary may resign at any time upon written notice to the president. The top circle may remove any officer from his or her executive office at any time without necessarily removing him or her from the top circle. Such removal shall be without prejudice to the contractual rights of such officer, if any, with the LLC.

Any number of executive offices may be held by the same person unless prohibited by governing law. The top circle at any regular or special meeting may fill any executive officer vacancy occurring in any office of the LLC by death, resignation, removal, or otherwise for the unexpired portion of the term.

3.2 Power to Require Security

The top circle may require any of its members, and any officer, agent, working member, or employee of the LLC to give security for the faithful performance of his or her duties.

ARTICLE 4 CIRCLE MANAGEMENT

4.1 General Provisions

Management of all circles of the LLC with the exception that management of the top circle shall be in accordance with the following procedures only to the extent that such procedures are not inconsistent with Article 2 or Article 3 hereof, or any other provisions of this operating agreement, the articles of organization, or the laws of [name of jurisdiction].

4.1.1 Circle Regulations

Each circle shall be a separate organ of the LLC and shall be empowered to draft its own regulations with respect to the tasks, authority, and responsibilities of the circle, which regulations shall not be in conflict with this operating agreement or any regulations that the top circle may adopt.

4.1.2 Assisting Circles

A circle is authorized to form assisting (or helping) circles to prepare decision-making recommendations for the circle. The assisting circle may be composed of persons from the circle, other circles, and external advisors.

4.1.3 Circle Decisions and Limits

Circles may make decisions within certain limits agreed on in the next higher circle; individual members may make independent decisions within the limits drawn up by their own circles.

4.2 Decision Making

4.2.1 The Principle of Consent

Decision-making shall be in accordance with the principle of consent or "no objection." Decision making does not require consent to be used for every decision of the circle, however, but it must be used to establish an alternative means of decision making for a specific decision or for a specific class of decisions.

4.2.2 Objections

Should there be a paramount objection to a decision, arguments for the objection must be given. An objection without reasoned argument will not be considered.

4.2.3 Second Meetings

If a circle is unable to reach a decision on a particular matter, a new meeting of the circle shall be convened after at least forty-eight (48) hours, with the same subject on the agenda.

4.2.4 Referring Decisions

If a circle is unable to reach a decision on a particular matter in a second meeting of the circle, the chairperson may refer the matter to the next higher or lower circle for decision or recommendation.

4.2.5 Annual Decision-Making Audit

An independent auditor shall review the decision-making process in each circle annually and shall report to the top circle whether the decision making of the circles conforms to this operating agreement.

4.2.6 Assuming Decision-Making Authority

The next higher circle is responsible for assuring that decision making in a circle functions according to this operating agreement. If the next higher circle concludes that the decision-making within a circle does not function according to this agreement, the next higher circle may take over the decision making of that circle on an interim basis.

The circle shall continue to make recommendations to the next higher circle concerning its area of responsibility. The next higher circle shall take such action(s) as it deems necessary to re-establish the circle's performance according to sociocratic (dynamic self-governance) principles as soon as possible. The next higher circle shall restore decision-making authority to the circle as soon as either the next higher circle or the independent auditor determines that decision-making is functioning according to sociocratic (dynamic self-governance) principles.

4.3 Selection of Persons

4.3.1 Officers and Representatives

Each circle shall elect a chairperson (or facilitator) of circle meetings and a secretary from amongst its members. Each circle shall also elect one or more representatives of the circle in the next higher circle, whether or not that person is a member of the circle, provided the representative is in some way connected to the LLC. These elections shall be conducted annually, or as deemed necessary by the circle, at a meeting convened for this purpose, according to the consent principle and after open discussion.

4.3.2 Multiple Functions

Persons may fulfill more than one function at the same time, unless this could result in a statutory, operational, or legal incompatibility, provided that the operational leader (elected by the next higher circle) and the representative may not be the same person.

4.3.3 Procedures for Appointment and Dismissal

Each circle shall determine procedures for the appointment and dismissal of members of the circle, in accordance with the law, this operating agreement, and the articles of organization. A circle shall make decisions as to the appointment or dismissal of its members only after the person involved has been given an opportunity to present his or her arguments. However, the person involved may not participate in the making of this decision.

In the absence of a written agreement to the contrary between an individual working partner and the LLC, these procedures shall not constitute a contract between any person and the LLC and all working partners of the LLC shall continue as working partners at the will of the LLC.

4.3.4 Objections to Appointments or Dismissals

In the event a circle objects to the appointment of or seeks to dismiss a representative of the next lower circle, the circle shall submit objections to the next lower circle concerning the functioning of its representative in the circle. Should the consideration of these objections not result in consent between the higher circle and the next lower circle, the higher circle may deny the representative the right to represent the lower circle in the higher circle.

Such denial of representation is an extreme remedy and the higher circle should only undertake it as a final resort and should take all necessary action to restore representation of the next lower circle as soon as possible.

4.4 Circle Meetings

4.4.1 Frequency

Circles shall meet at regular intervals, at least six times per year.

4.4.2 Convening and Notice

Regular circle meetings shall be convened by the chairperson (or facilitator) of the circle. All members shall receive notice of the meeting, the agenda, and any relevant information necessary to make decisions on matters to be discussed at the meeting within a reasonable time prior to the meeting.

4.4.3 Special Meetings

The chairperson shall convene a special meeting within seven (7) days of a request therefore from any member of the circle.

Should the chairperson fail to convene such a meeting within seven (7) days after the receipt of such a request, the circle member who made the request may convene the meeting.

4.4.4 Members Present (Quorum)

It is not necessary for all the members of the circle to be present to hold a meeting, however, consent is required from all members of a circle before a decision can take effect. Each circle shall establish its own written policy defining a quorum for conducting business and its procedures for obtaining consent from absent members.

4.4.5 Delegation of Participation

Members who are unable to be present can delegate their right to participate in decision making to another member of the circle. The right to participate, however, does not constitute a proxy consent or veto. The delegated right to participate is the right to present arguments on behalf of another circle member.

4.4.6 Recording Decisions

Any decision made during a circle meeting shall be recorded in circle minutes or notes to be circulated to all members of the circle and to other circles with which the circle is linked within three (3) days of the meeting in the format determined by the organization.

4.4.7 Amending or Repealing a Delegated Decision

Amending or repealing a delegated decision is possible provided the consent of the circle involved has been obtained.

ARTICLE 5 COMPENSATION AND PROFIT SHARING

5.1 Fixed Compensation

Both investing partners and working partners engaged in active operations shall receive fixed compensation to be reimbursed only from earnings from operations. The fixed part of the investing partners' reimbursement will be calculated at the end of fiscal year at the then prevailing prime lending rate. Working partners will be reimbursed throughout the business year at a fixed rate analogous to wages or salaries.

5.2 Variable Compensation

Both investing partners and working partners will receive variable reimbursements to be reimbursed only from earnings from operations. The reimbursements will vary depending on profitability. Variable compensation will be in the form of short-term measurement (STM) and long-term measurement (LTM) payments. STM payments will be made only when profits for the month exceed the targeted profit percentage. If profits for a month fall below the targeted profit percentage, that shortfall must be covered before any STM payments can be made. LTM payments will be made once or twice annually at the discretion of the top circle.

5.3 Determining Fixed and Variable Payments

5.3.1 At least annually, the top circle shall determine the amount targeted for company reserves and the targeted profit percentage.

5.3.2 At least at the end of each fiscal year, the top circle or person(s) delegated by the top circle will normally deduct the targeted reserve from the profits, calculate the amount of fixed payments due to investors per Section 7.1, and subtract that amount and the amount of the targeted reserve from the profits available for variable payments to the parties. The variable payments, however, are so important to the measurement process, a key component of the LLC management, the top circle can choose to make variable payments before fully paying investors' fixed payments.

5.3.3 The top circle or person(s) delegated by the top circle will calculate an STM payment for the investing and working partners each month and an LTM payment once or twice a year.

5.3.4 The top circle shall decide whether to have the company pay taxes on retained earnings at the corporate tax rate or to pass all earnings through to the partners.

OTHER ARTICLES

[Additional articles may be necessary to address such issues as indemnification, conflict of interest, fiscal year, corporate seal, and so forth. Care must be taken to ensure that these clauses do not contradict or undermine the provisions of Articles 1 through 6.]

ARTICLE X MISCELLANEOUS

Amendment of This Operating Agreement

This operating agreement may be altered or repealed and new agreements made by the top circle applying the principle of consent in accordance with the provisions of these agreements, with a minimum of thirty (30) days notice to all members of the LLC including investing partners, working partners, and board of directors members of intent to amend this operating agreement. The purpose of such notice shall be to allow all levels of the circle structure, including the investing partners, time to call special meetings, if necessary, to deliberate, and to select representatives to attend the deliberations of the next higher circle.

ADDENDUM

CONDUCT OF MEETINGS OF INVESTING PARTNERS

Article 1 Meetings of Investing Partners

Meetings of investing partners shall be conducted in accordance with the sociocratic (dynamic self-governance) method. By consent, the investing partners may choose methods and structures of decision-making other than consent for a meeting of investing partners.

Article 2 Notice of Meetings

Whenever the investing partners are required or permitted to take any action at a meeting, a written notice of the meeting shall be given to investing partners which shall state the place, date, and hour of the meeting, and, in the case of a special meeting, the purpose or purposes for which the meeting is called. Unless otherwise provided by law, the articles of organization, or these operating agreements, the written notice of any meeting shall be given not less than ten (10) nor more than sixty (60) days before the date of the meeting to the investing partners. If mailed, such notice shall be deemed to be given when deposited in the email or mail, postage prepaid, directed to the investing partner at its address as it appears on the records of the LLC.

2.1 Annual Meeting of Investing Partners

The investing partners shall meet annually for the purpose of electing a representative(s) to the top circle and determining the date and time of the next meeting. Only persons who have made monetary investment in the LLC plus the CEO plus the representative(s) from the general circle to the top circle shall participate in said meeting.

2.2 Special Meetings of Investing Partners

Special meetings of the investing partners may be called with at least 15 days notice by one or more of the investing partners, CEO, or elected representative to the top circle. Only the investing partners, the CEO, and the representative(s) to the top circle from the general circle shall be entitled to participate in such meetings. Special meetings will be for the sole purpose of considering the removal and/or replacement of the investing partners' representative(s) to the top circle.

2.3 List of Investing Partners Entitled to Participate in Annual and Special Meetings of Investing Partners

The secretary of the top circle, upon notice of an annual or special meeting of the investing partners, shall prepare and make, at least ten (10) days before such meeting, a complete list of the investing partners entitled to participate in the meeting, arranged in alphabetical order, and showing the address of each investing partner and the percentage of equity registered in the name of each investing partner. Such list shall be open to the examination of any investing partner in a designated electronic location.

Article 3 Quorum

Except as otherwise provided by law, the articles of organization, or this operating agreement, at each meeting of the investing partners the presence in person or by electronic means of a person or persons representing at least one-half of the total investment in the LLC plus the CEO or a Representative of the general circle shall constitute a quorum. The investing partners may, at their sole discretion, form a legal entity.

Article 4 Organization of Investing Partners Meeting

Meetings of the investing partners shall be presided over by the CEO, by a representative of the general circle, or by another person elected at the meeting by consent. The meeting attendees shall elect a secretary or direct the CEO to appoint a person to act as secretary of the meeting.

Article 5   Participation in Meetings

Each investing partner in attendance shall be entitled to participate in the consent decision-making process in the investing partners meeting. Members who are unable to be present can delegate their right to participate in decision making to another member of the investing partner's circle. The right to participate, however, does not constitute a proxy to consent or veto. The delegated right to participate is the right to present arguments on behalf of another circle member.

Article 6 Fixing Date for Determination of Investing Partner of Record

6.1 Fixed Record Date

In order that the LLC may determine the investing partners entitled to notice of or to participation in any meeting of investing partners or any adjournment thereof; or entitled to receive payment of any funds or other distribution or allotment of any rights; or entitled to exercise any rights in respect of any change, conversion, or exchange of partnership equity; or for the purpose of any other lawful action, the top circle may fix a record date. The record date shall not precede the date upon which the resolution fixing the record date is adopted by the top circle. The record date

(a) shall not be more than sixty (60) nor less than ten (10) days before the date of the next scheduled meeting of the investing partners;

(b) nor in the case of any other action, it shall not be more than sixty (60) days prior to such other action.

6.2 No Fixed Record Date

If no record date is fixed,

(a) the record date for determining investing partners entitled to notice of or to participate at a meeting of investing partners shall be at the close of business on the day preceding the day on which the meeting is held;

(b) the record date for determining investing partners for any other purpose shall be at the close of business on the day preceding the day on which the top circle adopts the resolution relating thereto.

A determination of investing partners of record entitled to notice of or to participate at a meeting of investing partners shall apply to any adjournment of the meeting; provided, however, that the top circle may fix a new record date for the adjourned meeting.

Article 7 List of Investing Partners Entitled to Participate

The person or persons responsible for calling an annual or special meeting of the investing partners must give the secretary of the top circle notice of the meeting at least fifteen (15) days in advance of the date of the meeting.

Guide for Circle Meetings

"The Cheat Sheet"

Circles, the basic governance unit in sociocratic organizations, are semi-autonomous, self-organizing groups of up to about 40 members, normally less, who share a common aim and thus constitute a *domain*. Circles make the policy decisions that govern the planing and execution of day-to-day operational functions and tasks that fall within their domain.

MEETING FORMAT

1. **Opening Round**

   A time to attune to each other and to the aim of the circle, similar to an orchestra tuning to one note before a performance.

2. **Administrative Concerns**

   Meeting support items that require little or no discussion or decisions. Announcements, consent to minutes of last meeting, date of next meeting, acceptance of the agenda, etc.

3. **Content**

   Agenda items (For example: Item 1, Item 2, etc.).

4. **Closing Round**

   Includes measurement and evaluation of the meeting and its results, and future agenda items.

CIRCLE MEMBERS & FUNCTIONS

Every member of the circle has a day-to-day "doing" function. In addition, some members have special roles in circle meetings. These functions are:

1. **Operational Leader**

    Supervises the circle's daily work. Elected by and participates in the next higher circle.

2. **Facilitator**

    Leads circle meetings. May or may not be the operational leader of the circle.

3. **Secretary**

    The circle administrator. Takes and publishes meeting minutes, announces and makes arrangements for meetings, collects items for the meeting agenda from other circle members, prepares handout materials, and prepares the agenda in consultation with the facilitator.

4. **Logbook Keeper**

    Often combined with secretary. Maintains records of minutes, policy decisions, detailed descriptions of work processes and instructions, financial records, etc.

5. **Elected Representative(s)**

    Represent(s) the circle in the next higher circle.

CONSENT PROCESS

Circles make policy decisions by consent, ensuring that all argued and paramount objections to a proposal have been addressed. The process varies depending on the complexity of the decision to be made.

Simple Consent

Simple consent can be used for approval of the minutes, assignment of a person to a previously consented task, etc.

1. **Facilitator Proposes a Policy**

2. **Consent Round**

    Facilitator asks for consent or arguments for paramount objections.

Consent to a Proposal (Short Format)

For a proposal, the process is more complex. Policy proposals are concrete strategies for meeting needs and should include the scope of the policy, what needs it addresses, and when possible, a time frame within which it will be reviewed.

1. **Present Proposal**

2. **Clarifying Questions (may be in a round)**

    Take questions related to understanding the proposal, not reactions.

3. **Quick Reactions**

   Brief observations, feelings, needs, alternative strategies, etc., related to the proposal. Usually in a round.

4. **Consent Round**

   In a round each person in turn consents or states paramount objections. The facilitator working with the secretary modifies the proposal as necessary. Repeat round with further amendments, if necessary.

Consent When Developing a Proposal (Long Format)

When no proposal is present, the process is even more complex with several steps.

Information Gathering (Input, also called "Picture Forming")

1. Explain the need or aim.

2. Identify, question, explore issues.

3. Consent to issues.

Proposal Development (Transformation)

4. Do round to collect ideas.

5. Combine ideas and draft a proposal.

6. Confirm that the draft proposal addresses all the issues.

Consent Round (Output)

7. Secretary and/or facilitator prepares and reads exact wording.

8. Consent round.

9. Announce decision (and celebrate).

DEFINING THE WORK PROCESS OF THE CIRCLE

Conceptually, the vision and mission are larger than the aim which has a more narrow focus, but it is generally easier to start designing the work process by beginning with the aim.

1. **Define the Aim**

   Describe the product or service, as differentiated from other products and services. Write the aim in terms the client, customer, or recipient will easily understand.

2. **Determine the Vision**

   Dreams of a better world and values with which the circle members identify. Visions are typically outward looking.

3. **Determine the Mission**

   What will the circle do to realize the vision. The overall mission motivates the circle to action. The mission is typically inward looking.

4. **Plan the Work Process**

   This makes the aim concrete.

   a. **Layout the "doing" in terms of all input, transformation, and output steps.**

   b. **Create the steering network of leading and measuring.**

      For each step in the doing process establish the governing policies that will guide the work and the methods of measuring its results.

   c. **Elect people by consent for each function and task.**

      Includes all leading, doing, and measuring steps.

   d. **Plan for development**

      This includes researching, learning, and teaching for each person and in interaction with each step in the doing process and in the steering network of leading and measuring.

Guide to the Implementation Process

Implementing and using the sociocratic method is a process of testing, evaluating, and retesting. In other words, the steps are to plan a step, try it out, evaluate how it worked, and adjust the plan. To begin:

1. Form an implementation circle that includes key decision-makers and representatives different levels of the organization. The implementation circle should:

   a. Define aim and circle structure

   b. Decide which circle(s) will be activated first

   c. Arrange training for members of first activated circles

   d. Develop in-house trainer(s)

   e. Establish a system for maintaining and developing the circle structure

   f. Develop a remuneration system in which everyone feels both the profits and the losses

2. If not activated first, activate the top circle. A complete top circle consists of outside experts, the managing officers, and representatives of the general circle. Some legal entities may be required to have a separate board of directors and if so, the members of the board may include the outside experts. If not they should be added to the top circle.

   Experts from outside the organization, usually four, represent:

   a. Legal advisor or representative of local government

   b. Expert in finance

   c. A social or management expert

   d. Expert on the aim of the organization

Additional members from the organization:

a. The chief executive officer (CEO), chief operations officer (COO), deputy officers, general manager(s), etc., (titles as appropriate to the organization)

b. Elected representative(s) from the general circle

3. The top circle, among other things, should:

a. Elect or affirm the chief executive officer

b. Adopt or affirm the aim statement, overall budgets, and policy plans

c. Determine the form of incorporation and by-laws

d. In a generative way, for example, proactively creating new ideas, connect the organization's aim to the environment

e. Exercise legally mandated fiduciary responsibilities

4. Once the circle structure is in place, dissolve the implementation circle. Some members of the circle may become internal trainers for the rest of the organization.

APPENDIX H

Guide for Logbooks

❧

Concept

Logbooks ensure that all members of the organization have the key records they need to do their work. Logbooks serve as the circle's short and long term memory system and like your own personal memory, updating must occur routinely. Each circle and each circle member should have a logbook that reflects a different place and perspective in the organization. As such, each person's unique logbook overlaps with the logbooks of others.

Maintenance

As a member of an organization you should maintain your own logbook. If you belong to more than one circle, you should keep the records from each circle in your logbook. The operational leader of each circle is responsible for the logbook of the circle, which is maintained with the help of the circle secretary and/or logbook keeper. Out-of-date logbook material should be retained for later reference.

Format

Each logbook has a common part that is the same for every circle and a specific part that is different for each circle and for each individual in the circle.

1. **Common content in all logbooks:**

    Statement of the organization's vision, mission, and aim(s)

    Bylaws

    Strategic policy plan

    Diagram of the circle organization

2. **Rules and Procedures**

    The general circle and all sub-circle logbooks should contain the rules and procedures approved by the general circle that apply to the whole organization.

Each circle logbook should also include all the rules and procedures the circle needs to accomplish its aim. The general circle logbook should include copies of all those circle-specific procedures.

The top circle logbook does not need the kind of operational detail kept in the general circle logbook, but it does need the complete text of the articles of incorporation and any related legal documents.

3. **Meeting Records**

    Each circle logbook and the logbook of each person in a circle should have a complete set of meeting decisions and/or records.

4. **Circle Members and their Work**

    The logbook should contain the names of all members of the circle and their functions, tasks, and responsibilities. It should also identify the chair, the secretary and/or logbook keeper, and the elected representative(s) to the next higher circle and their terms in those offices. This section should also include flow charts summarizing the leading, doing, and measuring activities of the circle.

5. **Circle Development Plan**

    Development includes any training, experience, teaching, and research that members of the circle need to function effectively in the circle. The circle chair is responsible for organizing development activities for circle members. Training is needed in:

    Knowledge and skills required to accomplish the circle's aim

    Decision-making methods

    Methods of organizing work and work processes

6. **Individual Work Plan**

    Your own logbook should include a description of the functions, tasks, and responsibilities for which you are responsible including:

    A summary of the work process for the your specific assignments

    Flow charts of your work

    Your unique development plan

A Guide to Elections by Consent

Circles elect their members to functions and tasks by consent following an open nominations process that includes arguments to support the nominations. Normally, the facilitator conducts elections.

1. **Define the Function or Task**

   Consent to or reaffirm a description of the function or task including the length of service and the means of measuring performance.

2. **Nominations**

   Submit written nominations containing the name of the nominator and the name of the person nominated for the task to the facilitator. A member of the circle may nominate any other member of the circle, him- or herself, or indicate "no nomination" or "outside hire."

   Nominations Form:

   ```
   [Your Name ]
   nominates
   [Nominee's Name ]
   ```

3. **Presentations**

   The facilitator reads the nomination form and asks each nominator for the reasons (arguments) for their nomination.

4. **Changes**

    The facilitator asks the nominators if they want to change their nominations based on other arguments. This can be done in a round or be a simple invitation to change. Nominations can then be revised or new nominations made. The facilitator ensures that nominators give their arguments for their changes.

5. **Consent**

    Based on the arguments given, the facilitator chooses a person from those nominated, giving a rationale for the choice, and asks each participant, in turn, if they consent to the proposed person, asking the proposed person last.

    If there is an argued and paramount objection, the circle may try to resolve the objection or may repeat the request for changes, resulting in a different proposed person. If there is a argued and paramount objection, the process repeats from step 4, "Changes," until there is a choice with no objections.

    If there are paramount objections to all the nominees, including objections by the nominees themselves, the circle continues to have a vacant function or task until the process is successfully completed. Normally, the operational leader is responsible for initiating and handling the process of hiring from the outside.

    Completing the process may require redefining the task description to address objections or hiring new circle members with the required knowledge and skills.

Cautions:

1. Specify term limits; do not elect for an unlimited term.

2. Listen without discussion or comment during the presentations.

3. Keep all options open as long as possible. That is, do not ask for volunteers nor ask who is interested.

4. Remember that choices are "more or less." No one will be perfect and everyone can learn. Do not look for the perfect candidate.

GLOSSARY OF SOCIOCRATIC TERMS

Many of these terms and definitions are based on the SCN 500 standards published by the Sociocratisch Centrum. Some are not discussed in the text because they refer to more complex processes than we were able to cover in the space available. We included the definitions, however, because they are instructive and not easily accessible elsewhere.

A B

aim. A product, service, or result that will enable an organization to realize its **vision** and **mission**. Unlike the vision and mission that address desired conditions, the aim is defined in terms of the **exchange object**. Also see **exchange relationship**.

aim realization. The process of achieving the aim. In sociocratic organizations, both the **primary process** and **supporting processes** are designed to ensure aim realization.

argued, arguments. Presented as or reasoned statements of fact, as in mathematical arguments. Depending on the context arguments may refer to any condition. An argument, for example, can presented initially as an uncomfortable feeling. In order for the circle to resolve objections they must be clearly expressed. One role of a skilled **facilitator** is to help circle members clarify arguments. See also the **principle of consent** and **paramount objections**.

assisting circle. See **helping circle**.

audit. See **sociocratic audit**.

autocratic decision-making. A decision-making method in which an individual or a small group of individuals makes decisions that affect or are binding on everyone else.

basis rule. Literal translation of the Dutch term *basis regeling*. See **governing principles**.

base wage. See **Guaranteed Base Wage (GBW)**.

both-and. Most often used as "both-and thinking." Incorporates and goes beyond "either-or thinking" to mean inclusive solutions that address the concerns of both parties, or all parties seeking solutions.

⇒ C ⇐

chairperson. Some circles may have an **operational leader** whose title is "chairperson." The chairperson may or may not be the same person as the circle meeting **facilitator.**

chaotic decision-making. A decision-making method in which unpredictable elements, often appearing to be random, self-organize to determine outcomes. See also **self-organizing systems.**

circle. A group of individuals within a sociocratic organization who share a common aim, such as a department, committee, or team. A circle is **semi-autonomous** and **self-organizing.** It sets its own policies within its **domain,** maintains its own memory system or **logbook,** and assumes responsibility for its own **development.** Circles are **double-linked** with leaders and representatives participating in the next higher circle to form the **governance structure** of a sociocratic organization.

The circle makes the link between individual identity and group identity. In the circle the interests of the individual and the interests of the group become mutual concerns.

circle decision. A decision reserved for the **circle** and made in **circle meetings.** Also see **policy decisions.**

circle meeting. A formal gathering of circle members to conduct the business of the **circle.** Circle meetings are generally held every 2-6 weeks and at least six times a year.

circle meeting leader. See **chairperson** and **facilitator.**

circle representative(s). See **representative(s).**

circle structure. The governance structure in a sociocratic organization that performs the **leading** and **measuring** functions in the **circular process** of leading-doing-measuring and reflects the **operational structure** that performs the **doing** function. Also see **circle, double-links,** and **governance structure.**

circular process. The functions of **leading-doing-measuring** used to guide or steer a sociocratic organization's governance and operations. See also **circle structure** and **input-transformation-output.**

closed system. An organization that has no structured relationship with its environment and thus lacks the information necessary to adapt to a changing environment. Sociocratic organizations are purposely structured as **open systems.**

closing round. A **round** completed at the end of a **circle meeting** in which each person is given an opportunity to make final comments. It often includes an evaluation of the meeting in terms of its productivity, relationship to aim realization, etc. Also see **opening round**.

compensation. Wages or other benefits received in exchange for services rendered. Compensation in a sociocratic organization consists of the **Guaranteed Base Wage** (GBW), the **Short Term Measurement** (STM) and the **Long-Term Measurement** (LTM). While the GBW is generally calculated based on market rates, the STM and LTM are variable based on profits and distributed to all employees. This structure ensures both a basic income and an income based on performance. The variable payments provide a measurement of the effectiveness and compensate all members of the organization as co-entrepreneurs.

consent. Consent is granted by an individual when all their **argued and paramount objections** to a proposed action have been satisfied. Consent is assumed if there are no objections raised. See also **principle of consent**.

consent round. A **round** in which the circle members, in turn, explicitly indicate their **consent** to a proposed decision because any **paramount and argued objections** have been resolved.

consensus. The state of having achieved the individual **consent** of each member of a **circle** or group. It does not imply agreement or **solidarity** but only that a proposed decision is the best one that can be achieved under the circumstances.

cybernetics. The science of communications and control whose principles were formulated by Norbert Weiner. An early expression of ideas that developed into systems thinking. Endenburg used cybernetics principles to analyze technical systems and, thinking by analogy, applied them to human systems to develop the sociocratic principles.

D

decision confirmation round. See **consent round**.

democratic governance. The governance structure of an organization functioning as a democracy, as opposed to a monarchy or a theocracy, in which the decision-making power is vested in its members collectively. In practice, members make decisions in democratic organizations by majority vote or delegate decisions to officers or representatives who are elected by majority of vote.

development. A process involving researching, teaching, and learning. Each circle is responsible for its own development and the development of its members. See also **sociocratic engineering**. In early sociocratic literature was referred to related concepts of "integral education," "permanent education," and "schooling."

domain. An area of authority or responsibility. The limits of the circle's domain are set by the next higher circle. The limits of a person's domain are set by the **circle**.

double-link, double-linking. The linking of a circle with the next higher circle in such a way that at least two persons, being the **operational leader** of that circle and at least one **representative** from that circle, are members of the next higher circle. The double-link (1) makes attuning between circles possible, (2) facilitates top down and bottom up communication, and (3) makes a **circular process** possible between circles.

double-linked circles. Related circles in the organization's governance structure. All circles in the organization are linked to the next higher circle by **double-links** that form a structure of linked circles. See also the **circle structure**.

dynamic. Of or pertaining to the ability to change. Not static. In physics, a dynamic element is one that is unstable, changing. See **dynamic steering**.

dynamic governance, dynamic self-governance. Alternative names for **sociocracy** that reflect its use of **dynamic steering** in applying the **circular process** to the governance of the organization.

dynamic steering. A governing process that can self-correct in response to its changing environment. See also **circular process**.

⇒ E ⇐

election of people to functions and tasks. The fourth principle applies the principle of consent to the assignment of functions and tasks: People are elected to functions and tasks by consent after open nominations. Also referred to as a *sociocratic election*.

enfranchised. To be free, or set free. To have legal voting rights. To control one's own destiny. All members of a sociocratic organization are enfranchised.

equivalence. The equal valuing of each individual, in distinction to valuing, for example, the majority or the management more highly. See also **principle of consent** and **round**.

exchange object. The object, service, or financial compensation to be provided or obtained in an **exchange relationship**. See also **aim**.

exchange partner. An organization or person with whom **exchange objects** are traded. See **exchange relationship**.

exchange process. The trading of goods and services based on mutual agreements. See also **exchange relationship**.

exchange relationship. A relationship between parties who trade goods or services based on mutual agreements. In sociocracy, the **principle of consent** rules exchanges and emphasis is placed on the synergistic effects of mutually profitable exchanges and on developing **exchange partners**.

execution of policy. Process of implementing **circle** decisions. The circle delegates execution to its members, the **operational structure**, and to **linked circles**.

Existence Possibility Guarantee (EPG). See **Guaranteed Base Wage**.

external financial or **economic expert.** A member of the **top circle,** who has professional connections and knowledge of developments in the economic and financial field relevant to the organization's aim.

external legal expert. A member of the **top circle**, who has professional connections and knowledge of developments in the legal field relevant to the organization's **aim**.

external social or **organizational expert.** A member of the **top circle**, who has professional connections and knowledge of developments in the social or organizational field relevant to the organization's **aim**.

external expert in the organization's aim or field of operation. A member of the **top circle**, who has professional connections and knowledge of developments in the areas relevant to the organization's **aim**, the organization's **exchange objects**, and **exchange partners**.

⇒ F ⇐

facilitator. One of the four circle officers. The circle meeting leader. Each circle selects one of its members to lead or facilitate their circle meetings. The facilitator works with the circle **secretary** and **logbook keeper** to determine agendas and ensure the integrity of the circle's functioning, maintains the **memory system,** and oversees the process of policy development. The facilitator, as leader of the meeting, is not necessarily the same person as the **operational leader** but may be.

feedback loops. Elements in an organization or other system that provide information about how the organization is performing. See also **dynamic steering** and **circular process**.

feed-forward loops. Elements in an organization or other system that use given measurements to control future responses to environmental events. See also **dynamic steering** and **circular process**.

four governing principles. See **governing principles**.

free organization. A fully sociocratic organization is not owned by anyone; it owns itself. There are various legal structures in which this can be accomplished in corporations including an LLC. Another strategy, a double corporation may be used to place ownership of controlling stock in a foundation whose board is identical to that of the company to ensure that consent is the ultimate basis of decision making, not ownership.

⇒ G ⇐

governance structure. The structure used to steer an organization toward its aims. This structure determines who, when, and how decisions will be made, including **aim realization**. In autocratic organizations, the owner or a board of directors is given this power. In democratic organizations, it is given to the majority of members who generally elect officers and/ or a board that make decisions. In sociocratic organizations, governance decisions are made by all members of the organization through the **circle structure** and the **principle of consent**.

governing principles, the four governing principles. Sociocratic governance is based on four principles:

1. **Consent** governs decision making. Consent means there are no **argued and paramount objections** to a proposed **policy decision**.

2. The context for consent decision-making is the **circle**, a **semi-autonomous** and **self-organizing** group of individuals who govern their own work within their assigned **domain**. A circle has its own **aim**, delegates the functions of **leading, doing**, and **measuring** to its own members, and maintains its own **memory system** and program of **development**.

3. Circles are interconnected by a **double-link** consisting of the **operational leader** and one or more **representatives** who participate fully in the decision making of the next higher circle.

4. Circles **elect people to functions and tasks** by consent after open nominations.

Guaranteed Base Wage (GBW). A level of **compensation** that may include goods, services, education, and wages that is determined by a circle and available to every member of that circle. The GBW is a prerequisite for safety in applying the principle of **consent** because it ensures a basic level of compensation. Also referred to as an *Existence Possibility Guarantee (EPG)*.

⇒ H I ⇐

helping circle. A temporary **circle** established for the preparation of a **policy decision** proposal. A helping circle may consist of members of the same circle; members of other circles; and/or members from social sectors linked to the organization by external experts. A helping circle does not determine policy. Also called an *assisting circle*.

hierarchy. An arrangement of persons or things in grades, orders, or classes, one above another in order to understand or illustrate their operational or developmental relationships to each other. Each level of a hierarchy represents a different level of abstraction and range of decision making. Each level is different in kind, not importance.

Hierarchies are evident in all natural systems. Sociocratic hierarchies, like natural hierarchies, include bottom up as well as top down communications and control. Autocratic hierarchies, by comparison, are top down only and typically illustrate **power-over** relationships rather than operational relationships. The principles of **consent** and **double-linked circles** enable a sociocratic hierarchy to use a circular process.

ignoring as violence. Ignoring individuals is regarded in sociocratic institutions as a form of violence, and possibly the ultimate source of all violence. Requiring the **consent** of each individual within a **domain** of decision-making makes it impossible to ignore individuals, thus avoiding this form of violence.

incentive, short term and long term. See **Short-Term Measurement (STM)** and **Long-Term Measurement (LTM)**.

integral education. See **development**.

input. The first step in determining the organization's **exchange relationship** with its environment. See also **input-transformation-output**.

input-transformation-output. The process that guides the production of a product or service. Simply put, one obtains an order (input), makes the product or provides the service (transformation), and receives compensation (output). See also **exchange process**.

integral education. See **development**.

⇒ J K L ⇐

linked circles. See **double-linked circles**.

logbook. The logbook functions as the **memory system** of the **circle** and each individual member of the organization. It serves the **measuring** function in the **circular process** of **leading-doing-measuring**. It contains all the **policy decisions**, meeting notes, and other data important to the functioning of the circle and to measuring the results of its decisions. Each circle member also has a logbook that contains both the circle's records and the records relating to their own work.

logbook keeper. One of the officers of a **circle**. Is responsible for keeping the circle's **logbook** up to date. Often combined with the role of the circle **secretary**.

Long Term Measurement (LTM). Part of the **compensation** in a sociocratic organization based on long term profits, generally distributed semi-annually or annually. Also see **compensation, Guaranteed Base Wage (GBW),** and **Short Term Measurement (STM).**

leading-doing-measuring. The three functions of the **circular process** on which the sociocratic **circle structure** is based. See also **leading, doing, measuring,** and **feedback** and **feed-forward loops.**

⇒ M N O ⇐

magical decision-making. See **theocratic decision-making.**

measuring. One function of the **steering process** of **leading-doing-measuring.** The process of producing information from the data compiled during the **doing** or execution function that will be required for evaluation in the next function, **leading.**

measurement. Compensation in a sociocratic organization is partly based on measuring the results of the work of the organization. See **Short Term Measurement (STM)** and **Long-Term Measurement (LTM).**

memory system. See **logbook.**

mission or **mission statement.** A written statement that explains what the organization intends to do to realize its **vision** of the future. The mission statement is a source of internal motivation. Also see **vision,** which focuses on the external environment and provides the organization's identity, and **aim,** which represents an exchange of the outside and inside.

nine-block chart, plan. A diagram of nine blocks for planning a **doing** process. It combines the three **leading-doing-measuring** functions (vertically) with the **input-transformation-output** processes (horizontally). See *Chapter Twelve: Organizing Work* for an example.

notetaker. See **secretary.**

objection. An argument against a proposed decision, stated clearly enough to be resolved. In sociocratic organizations, **consent** is based on the absence of **argued and paramount objections.**

open system. An organization linked to its environment. An open system has the ability to self-correct and self-renew, as opposed to a **closed system** that will inevitably decline due to entropy and cannot self-correct in response to its environment. Also see **dynamic steering.**

opening round. A **round** that begins the **circle meeting.** Members attune themselves to the **aim** of the **circle** as they share feelings, expectations, potential agenda issues, etc. Roughly analogous to an orchestra tuning to a note. This focuses circle members on their common interest which is the basis for **consent decision-making.**

operational decisions. Decisions affecting the day-to-day operations of the organization. Operational decisions are governed by **policy decisions**

made by the **circle structure** and are normally delegated to the operational leader.

operational leader. The circle member responsible for day-to-day **operational decisions** in the circle's **domain**. See also **operational structure**.

operational structure. The structure of the organization that performs the **doing** function in the **circular process** of leading-doing-measuring. The operational structure reflects the **circle structure** that performs the **leading** and **measuring** functions.

output. The third step in the **input-transformation-output** process in which the client or customer receives the product or service and makes a payment for it, completing the **exchange process**.

⇒ P Q ⇐

paramount. Of overriding importance, as in **argued** and paramount **objections**. A paramount objection is one that would prevent a circle member from being able to work toward the **aim** of his or her circle. Also see the **principle of consent**.

pattern language. Sociocratic norms are formulated as a pattern language, which is a structured method of describing good design practices within a particular domain. In addition to naming the processes and elements, describing effective solutions, and structuring solutions in a logical way, pattern languages allow designers to construct many models using the same methods and processes.

Pattern languages formalize decision-making values and structure fundamentally complex systems without oversimplification. The structure and pattern reveal the inter-relationships between processes and functions as part of the larger whole.

policy, policy decision, policy determination, policy plan. A decision or group of decisions that govern or constrain future **operational decisions**. A policy sets aims, standards, and limits. It may allocate resources, clarify values, establish plans, or specify general procedures. Policy decisions are the responsibility of the **circle,** as opposed to **operational decisions** that may be delegated to the **operational leader,** and are made by the **circles** in the **domain** they affect by **consent**. In sociocratic organizations, policies are written for a specific period of time after which they must be evaluated. Policies may be reviewed whenever circumstances change or there is new information to consider.

policy execution. Once a **circle** has completed a **policy** plan or document, it can delegate execution to its own members, the **operational structure**, or to lower, **linked circles**. Normally, policy execution requires strategic and tactical plans. See **strategic planning process** and **tactics**.

policy preparation. The process of developing a **policy** proposal that may be delegated to an **assisting** or **helping circle.**

power-over. An autocratic concept in which one person or group dominates another. Also see **power-with.**

power-with. A concept of power as shared. In sociocratic organizations the circle structure and the principle of consent ensures that power is shared and cannot become "**power over.**"

primary process. The operations directly related to realizing an **aim**, in generating a service or product, in contrast to a **secondary process** such as marketing or human resources that support delivery or production. An organization can engage in several primary processes. Also see **exchange process.**

principle of consent. The first organizing principle in sociocracy: *The principle of consent governs decision making.* In sociocratic organizations, all members must consent to **policy decisions** made by their **circle.** This is the primary mechanism for maintaining **equivalence** between all members of an organization. It also ensures greater commitment to the organization and that all available information has been considered before a decision is made.

⇒ R ⇐

representative(s). A **circle** member or members, but not the **operational leader,** chosen by the circle to participate in the decision making in the next higher circle. Representatives participate in decision making without instruction or consultation; they are full participants and decision makers, not vote carriers.

reaction round. A quick **round** in which each member of the circle gives a one or two word response to a proposed decision. Used to quickly determine if a proposal is ready for discussion or **consent.**

ring. English translation of the Dutch word *kring.* See **circle.**

round. A process in a meeting in which each member in turn is given an opportunity to speak. Doing a round maintains or reestablishes **equivalence** after a period of open discussion or when beginning or closing a meeting. See also **opening round, closing round, reaction round,** and **consent round.**

⇒ S ⇐

secretary. Circle officer who is responsible for the administration of the circle's decision-making process. Includes collecting agenda items and documents for circle meetings, distributing the agenda and documents to circle members, taking notes of the meeting, and distributing decisions. This function is often combined with the **logbook keeper** in smaller circles.

self-organizing systems. A concept arising from chaos theory where natural systems are found to emerge out of chaos into organized patterns. In sociocracy it is used to refer to the expectation that **circles** and individuals will organize their own work.

semi-autonomous. As in "circles are semi-autonomous and self-organizing." Within the policies of the larger organization, circles set their own policies and determine how they will function on a day-to-day basis.

Short Term Measurement (STM). Part of the **compensation** in a sociocratic organization based on profits, generally distributed several times a year or when a project is completed. Also see **Guaranteed Base Wage (GBW)** and **Long-Term Measurement (LTM)**.

sociocracy. An inclusive method of **governance** based on the **equivalence** of all members of the organization. Equivalence is ensured by the principle of consent. Steerability of the organization is assured through circular processes.

sociocratic audit. A systematic and independent examination to determine if the activities and results of an organization are in accordance with sociocratic methods, and if it has been implemented efficiently. See **sociocratic auditor.**

sociocratic auditor. Person who is qualified to execute sociocratic audits.

sociocratic certificate. Written document stating that the organization or person is in compliance with a certain sociocratic norm. See **sociocratic audit** and **sociocratic certification.**

sociocratic certification. A guarantee of compliance with a particular sociocratic norm. Granted to organizations and persons with specific sociocratic competencies.

Sociocratic Circle-Organization Method (SCM). The formal name of what is called by various names in North America including sociocracy, dynamic governance, dynamic self-governance, biodynamic governance, direct democracy, and sociocratic governance. SCN 500 defines this as "A compilation of rules and procedures that make it possible for people as unique persons to work and live together in equivalence." See also **governing principles.**

sociocratic compensation system. See **compensation.**

sociocratic election. See **election of people** to functions and tasks.

sociocratic engineering. Analysis, design, construction, deconstruction, and planning for development of an organization based on sociocratic principles and methods.

sociocratic hierarchy. A sociocratic hierarchy consists of a structure of interlinked circles that compose the governance structure in a sociocratic organization. In contrast to autocratic hierarchies, this structure is one of communications and control, a steering mechanism, that is based on a **power-with**. Also see **hierarchy.**

sociocratic norm. Sociocratic norms are established, published, and revised by the circles of the Sociocratisch Centrum in The Netherlands (SCN) based on the understanding that unambiguous definitions enhance the successful transmission of **sociocracy**. These norms also state the arguments that apply to the norms, allowing for criticism and subsequent improvement of the sociocratic method. See also **pattern language.**

sociocratic organization or **company.** A legal entity with (1) the **governing principles** of **sociocracy** incorporated into its statutes, bylaws, or operating agreements, and (2) a separation of ownership and authority structure, in other words, a **free organization.**

sociocratic consultant. Person certified to advise organizations about the introduction and implementation of the sociocratic method.

sociocratic trainer. Person qualified to teach the sociocratic method.

sociocratic structure. In the sociocratic method, the structure of an organization is "a configuration of transformation points which, as a whole, has the characteristic of letting specific processes take place." In other words, the structure reveals the points at which change, transformation, can happen.

solidarity. A total or high level of commitment to a shared aim that is often required by resistance fighters or other groups engaging in life threatening risks. Sometimes confused with **consensus.**

strategy. A choice amongst alternatives that an organization makes in order to execute its policies. See also **strategic planning process.**

strategic planning process. A long-term, all-encompassing plan that describes the methods and means that an organization has chosen to use in order to carry out its policies. In a sociocratic organization, the strategic planning process, like the governance process, includes the whole organization and is conducted by the circle structure. See also **tactics.**

steering. Governing. Also refers to the **circular process** of **leading-doing-measuring.** See **dynamic steering.**

supporting process(es). The organization's operations that function in support of the primary process of **aim** realization, for example, in creating the prerequisites to production.

system, systems theory, systems thinking. A system is a dynamic and complex whole that interacts as a structured functional unit. Systems are often composed of entities seeking equilibrium but can exhibit oscillating, chaotic, or exponential growth or decay.

⇒ T U ⇐

tactics. The short-term, day-to-day methods and means used to implement a longer term strategy. See **strategic planning process.**

theocratic decision-making. Method of decision making in which decisions are made on the basis of faith in a supernatural power or a given set of rules or beliefs that are unquestionable.

top circle. The top circle connects the organization to its environment preventing it from becoming a **closed system.** The top circle consists of the officers of the organization; elected **representive(s)** from the **general circle,** an **external financial** or **economic expert;** an **external legal expert;** an **external social or organizational expert;** and an **external expert on the purpose or operations of the organization.** The top circle complements the information gained by the organization in its **exchange relationships** by predicting changes in the environment and correcting the exchange relationship when necessary.

transformation. The second step in the process that guides production of a product or service. It creates the product or service by connecting or transforming assets such as land, labor, capital, and materials in to a new form. See **input-transformation-output.**

⇒ V W X Y Z ⇐

vision or vision statement. An organization's description of the future as desired by the organization. Distinct from the **mission** and **aim.** It may be described as the organization's dream for the future.

Bibliography

Ackoff, Russell Lincoln. 1989. "The Circular Organization." *Academy of Management Executive*, 3:11-16.

————. 1981. *Creating the Corporate Future: Plan or Be Planned.* NY: Wiley.

————. 1979. *The Democratic Organization.* NY: Oxford University Press.

Amar, Akhil Reed. 2005. *America's Constitution: A Biography.* NY: Random House.

Ansoff, Igor. 1956. *Corporate Strategy: An Analytical Approach to Business Policy for Growth and Expansion.* NY: McGraw-Hill. Revised edition: *The New Corporate Strategy.* NY: Wiley, 1989.

Argyris, Chris. 1957. *Personality and Organization: The Conflict Between the System and the Individual.* NY: Harper.

————. 1960. *Understanding Organizational Behavior.* Homewood, IL: Dorsey Press.

Avery, Michel, et al., 1981. *Building United Judgement: A Handbook for Consensus Decision Making.* The Center for Conflict Resolution. Reprinted by the Fellowship for Intentional Community, 1999.

Babbage, Charles. 1832. *On the Economy of Machinery and Manufacturers.* London: C. Knight.

Barnard, Chester I. 1938. *The Functions of the Executive.* Cambridge, MA: Harvard University Press.

Bennis, Warren. 1989. *Why Leaders Can't Lead: The Unconscious Conspiracy Continues.* San Francisco: Jossey-Bass. First edition: NY: AMACOM, 1976.

Blackwell, Christopher W. 2006. *Demos: Classical Athenian Democracy.*

A publication of The Stoa: a Consortium for Electronic Publication in the Humanities. http://www.stoa.org/projects/demos/home (Accessed August 2006).

Boeke, Kees. 1957. *Cosmic View: The Universe in 40 Jumps.* Introduction by Arthur H. Compton. NY: John Day, 1957. Available online at: http://www.vendian.org/mncharity/cosmicview/

———. 1945. "Sociocracy: Democracy as It Might Be" as edited by Beatrice C. Boeke. Online at: worldteacher.faithweb.com/sociocracy.htm (Accessed May 2007).

Bohm, David. 1980. *Wholeness and Implicate Order.* London; Boston: Routledge & Kegan Paul.

———, and B. J. Hiley. 1993. *The Undivided Universe: An Ontological Interpretation of Quantum Theory.* London: NY: Routledge.

Boulding, Kenneth. 1958. *Principles of Economic Policy.* Englewood Cliffs, NJ: Prentice-Hall.

———, 1950. *A Reconstruction of Economics.* NY: Wiley.

———. 1985. *The World as a Total System.* Beverly Hills, CA: Sage Publications.

Buck, John. 2003. "Employee Engagement in Sociocratic versus Conventional Organizations." Master's thesis. George Washington University.

———, and Gerard Endenburg. 1987. "The Creative Forces of Self-Organization." Paper published by the Sociocratisch Centrum, The Netherlands.

Buhl, J., et al., 2006. "From Disorder to Order in Marching Locusts." *Science*, 312: 1402-1406.

Burns, James MacGregor. 1978. *Leadership.* NY: Harper & Row.

Butler, C. T., and Amy Rothstein. 1991. *Conflict and Consensus: A Handbook of Formal Consensus Decisionmaking.* Second edition. Portland, ME: Food Not Bombs.

Chandler, Alfred. 1962. *Strategy and Structure: Chapters in the History of the Industrial Enterprise.* Cambridge: MIT Press.

———. 1980. *The Visible Hand: The Managerial Revolution in American Business.* Cambridge: Harvard University Press.

Chaplin, Charlie. 1936. *Modern Times.* Hollywood, CA: United Artists.

Silent film with synchronized soundtrack.

Charest, Gilles. 1996. *La Gestion par Consentement: Une Novelle Facon de Partager le Pouvoir [Management by Consent: A New Way of Sharing Power]*. Montreal: Les Editions Transcontinental.

———. 1988. *Du Manaagement à l'Écogestion* [Management by Consent]. Montreal: L. Courteau.

Clausewitz, Carl von. 1968. *On War.* Edited with an introduction by Anatol Rapoport. Mattituck, NY: Aeonian Press. Originally published as *Vom Kriege* 1832; first English translation, 1908.

Collins, Jim. 2001. *Good to Great: Why Some Companies Make the Leap ... and Others Don't.* NY: HarperCollins.

Comte, Auguste. 1853. *Positive Philosophy*. English translation of *Cours de Philosophie. Six volumes, 1830-1842.* Translated and condensed by Harriet Martineau.

Couzin, Iain D. 2005. "Effective Leadership and Decision-Making in Animal Groups on the Move." *Nature*, 433: 513-516.

Cyert, Richard and James March. 1963. *A Behavioral Theory of the Firm.* Englewood Cliffs, NJ: Prentice-Hall.

Deming. W. Edwards. 1984. *Chain Reaction: Quality, Productivity, Lower Costs, Capture the Market.* Cambridge, MA: MIT Center for Advance Engineering Study.

———. 1986. *Out of the Crisis.* Cambridge, MA: MIT Press

Dressler, Larry. 2006. *Consensus through Conversation: How to Achieve High-Commitment Decisions.* San Francisco: CA: Berrett-Koehler.

Drucker, Peter F. 1954. *The Practice of Management.* NY: Harper.

Eames, Charles and Ray. 1978. *The Powers of Ten: A Film Dealing with the Relative Size of Things in the Universe and the Effect of Adding Another Zero.* Based on the book *Power of Ten* by Kees Boeke. Made by the office of Charles and Ray Eames for IBM. Video Release: Santa Monica, CA: Pyramid Media.

Elliott, Jaques. 2002. *The Life and Behavior of Living Organisms: A General Theory.* Westport, CT: Praeger.

———. 1998. *Requisite Organization. A Total System for Effective Managerial Organization & Managerial Leadership for the 21st Century.* Revised second edition. Arlington, VA: Caslon Hall. Originally published 1986.

Endenburg, Gerard. 1974. *Dictatuur, Democratie, Sociocratie.* Rotterdam: Endenburg Elektrotechniek.

——. 1998. *Kennis, Macht en Overmacht: De Lerende Organisatie, in het Bijzonder de Sociocratische Kringorganisatie.* Delft: Eburon.

——. 1981. *Sociocratie : Het Organiseren van de Besluitvorming : een Waarborg voor Ieders Gelijkwaardigheid.* Alphen aan den Rijn: Samsom. English translation: *Sociocracy: The Organization of Decision-Making* (Delft: Eburon, 1998).

——. 1997. *Sociocratie als Sociaal Ontwerp in Theorie en Praktijk.* Delft: Eburon, 1997. Translated from the Dutch by Murray Pearson as: *Sociocracy as Social Design: Its Characteristics and Course of Development, as Theoretical Design and Practical Project* (Delft: Eburon, 1998).

——. 1975. *Sociocratie: Een Redelijk Ideaal [Sociocracy: A Reasonable Ideal].* Zaandijk [Lagedijk 169]: Woudt.

Feyerabend, Paul K.. 1975. *Against Method: Outline of an Anarchist Theory of Knowledge.* London: Humanities Press.

Fletcher, Ronald. 1971. *The Making of Sociology: A Study of Sociological Theory.* From a reprint of the original 1971 edition. 2 vols. Jaipur: Rawat Publications, 2000.

Follett, Mary Parker. 1940. *Dynamic Administration: The Collected Papers of Mary Parker Follett.* Edited by Henry C. Metcalf and L. Urwick. NY: London: Harper.

Gilbreth, Frank B., Jr., and Ernestine Gilbreth Carey. 1948. *Cheaper by the Dozen.* NY: Grossett & Dunlap.

——. 1950. *Cheaper by the Dozen.* Directed by Walter Lang. Hollywood, CA: 20th Century Fox. Film.

Haken, H[erman]. 1978. *Synergetics: An Introduction: Nonequilibrium Phase Transitions and Self-Organization in Physics, Chemistry, and Biology.* Springer Series in Synergetics, vol. 1. Berlin; NY: Springer-Verlag.

Hamel, Gary. 2000. *Leading the Revolution: How to Thrive in Turbulent Times by Making Innovation a Way of Life.* Cambridge, MA: Harvard University Press.

Holocaust Encyclopedia. "Joop Westereel." United States Holocaust Museum, http://www.ushmm.org (Accessed February 2007).

Jantsch, Erich. 1980. *The Self-Organizing Universe: Scientific and Human Implications of the Emerging Paradigm of Evolution.* Oxford; NY: Pergamon Press.

Jay, Antony. 1967. *Management and Machiavelli: An Inquiry into the Politics of Corporate Life.* London: Hodder & Stoughton.

Juran, J. M. 1964. *Managerial Breakthrough: A New Concept of the Manager's Job.* NY: McGraw-Hill. Revised edition: *Managerial Breakthrough: The Classic Book on Improving Management Performance* (NY: McGraw-Hill, 1995).

———. 1951. *Quality Control Handbook.* NY: McGraw Hill. Reprinted as *Juran's Quality Control Handbook* beginning in 1968.

———, and Frank M. Gryna, Jr. 1970. *Quality Planning and Analysis: From Product Development Through Use.* NY: McGraw-Hill.

Klarreich, Erica. 2006. "The Mind of the Swarm." *Science News,* 170:347.

Knight, Douglas E., and Herbert W. Robinson. 1972. *Cybernetics, Artificial Intelligence, and Ecology.* Proceedings of the Fourth Annual Symposium of the American Society for Cybernetics. NY: Spartan Books.

Koestler, Arthur. 1976. *Bricks to Babel.* First American edition. Includes a postscript by the author. NY: Random House.

———. 1980. *Bricks to Babel: A Selection from 50 Years of His Writings, Chosen with a New Commentary by the Author.* NY: Random House.

Likert, Rensis. 1967. *The Human Organization: Its Management and Value.* NY: McGraw-Hill.

———. 1961. *New Patterns of Management.* NY: McGraw-Hill.

———, and Jane Gibson Likert. 1976. *New Ways of Managing Conflict.* NY: McGraw-Hill.

Machiavelli, Niccolò. 1980. *The Prince.* Introduction by Christian Gauss. The Oxford University Press "World's Classics" translation by Luigi Ricci, revised by E. R. P. Vincent. NY: New American Library.

Manville, Brook, and Josiah Ober. 2003. "Beyond Empowerment: Building a Company of Citizens," *Harvard Business Review,* January.

Mayo, Elton. 1933. *The Human Problems of an Industrial Civilization.* NY: Macmillan.

Mooney, James D., and Alan C. Reiley. 1931. *Onward Industry! The*

Principles of Organization and Their Significance to Modern Industry.
NY: Harper & Brothers.

Morgan, Gareth. 1997. *Images of Organization.* Second edition. Thousand
Oaks, CA: Sage Publications.

Naisbitt, John. 1982. *Megatrends: Ten New Directions Transforming Our
Lives.* NY: Warner Books.

Nash, John F., Jr. 1997. "Equilibrium Points in n-Person Games." "The
Bargaining Problem." "Non-Cooperative Games." In *Classics in Game
Theory* edited by Harold W. Kuhn. Princeton, NJ: Princeton University
Press.

———. 1996. *Essays on Game Theory.* Cheltenham, UK: Brookfield, VT: E.
Elgar.

Nauta, D. 1984. *Defensie in Sociocratisch Perspectif.* Hoofdstuk 8 in M.H.K.
van der Graaf, *De crisis van de Technocratie en het alternatief van de
sociocratie.* De Horstink.

———, and E. van der Verlde. 1987. "Informatisering en arbeid." In
Wijsgerig Perspectief, 27:5, 156-162.

Ober, Josiah. 1989. *Mass and Elite in Democratic Athens: Rhetoric, Ideology,
and the Power of the People.* Princeton, NJ: Princeton University Press.

Ohmae, Kenichi. 1990. *The Borderless World: Power and Strategy in the
Interlinked Economy.* London: Collins.

———. 1995. *End of the Nation State: The Rise of Regional Economies.*
London: HarperCollins.

———. 1982. *The Mind of the Strategist: The Art of Japanese Business.* NY;
London: McGraw-Hill.

Owen, Robert. 1815. "Observations on the Effect of the Manufacturing
System." Reprinted in *The Voice of Toil: Nineteenth-Century British
Writing about Work* edited by David J. Bradshaw and Suzanne Ozment
(Athens, OH: Ohio University Press, 2000).

Pascale, Richard Tanner and Anthony G. Athos. 1981. *The Art of Japanese
Management: Applications for American Executives.* NY: Simon and
Schuster.

Peters, Tom, and Nancy Austin. 1985. *A Passion for Excellence: The
Leadership Difference.* NY: Random House.

———, and Robert H. Waterman, Jr. 1982. *In Search of Excellence: Lessons
from America's Best Run Companies.* NY: Harper and Row.

———. 1987. *Thriving on Chaos: Handbook for a Management Revolution.* NY: Knopf.

Prigogine, Ilya. 1997. *The End of Certainty: Time, Chaos, and the New Laws of Nature.* NY: Free Press.

———, and Isabelle Stengers. 1984. *Order Out of Chaos: Man's New Dialogue with Nature.* Toronto; NY: Bantam Books.

———. 1977. *Self-Organization in Nonequilibrium Systems: From Dissipative Structures to Order through Fluctuations.* NY: Wiley.

Quarter, Jack. 2000. *Beyond the Bottom Line: Socially Innovative Business Owners.* Westport, CT: Quorum Books.

Rapoport, Anatol. 1986. *General Systems Theory: Essential Concepts and Applications.* Tunbridge Wells Kent; Cambridge, MA: Abacus Press.

Rogers, Everett M. 2003. *Diffusion of Innovations.* Fifth edition. NY: Free Press.

Romme, A. Georges L. 1994. "Continuous Self-Renewal: The Case of Sociocracy." Research memorandum, RM/0/94-039. Maastricht: Maastricht Research School of Economics of Technology and Organizations.

———. 1996. "Making Organizational Learning Work: Consent and Double Linking Between Circles." *European Management Journal,* 14 (1): 69-75.

———. 1997. "Work, Authority, and Participation: The Scenario of Circular Organizing." *Journal of Organizational Change Management,* 10 (2):156-166.

———, and Gerard Endenburg. 2006. "Construction Principles and Design Rules in the Case of Circular Design." *Organization Science : a Journal of the Institute of Management Sciences.* 17 (2):287.

———, and Annewick J. M. Reijmer. *Sociocracy in Endenburg Elektrotechniek.* Winner of the 1995 European Case Writing Competition sponsored by the European Foundation for Management Development. Reprints available from the Sociocratisch Centrum.

Rosnay, Joël de. 1979. *The Macroscope: A New World Scientific System.* NY: Harper & Row.

Schein, Edgar H. 1997. *Organizational Culture and Leadership.* Second edition. San Francisco: Josssey-Bass.

Senge, Peter M. 1990. *The Fifth Discipline: The Art and Practice of the*

Learning Organization. NY: Doubleday.

Simon, Herbert A. 1957. *Administrative Behavior: A Study of Decision-Making Processes in Administrative Organization.* NY: Macmillan.

Sun-tzu. 1994. *The Art of War.* Translated with introduction by Ralph D. Sawyer with the collaboration of Mei-chün Lee Sawyer. Boulder, CO: Westview Press.

Surowiecki, James. 2004. *The Wisdom of Crowds: Why the Many Are Smarter Than the Few and How Collective Wisdom Shapes Business, Economies, Societies, and Nations.* NY: Doubleday.

Susskind, Lawrence and Jeffrey L. Cruickshank. 2006. *Breaking Robert's Rules: The New Way to Run Your Meeting, Build Consensus, and Get Results.* NY: Oxford University Press.

Taylor, Fredrick Winslow. 1911. *The Principles of Scientific Management.* NY: London: Harper.

Tuchman, Barbara. 1978. *A Distant Mirror: The Calamitous 14th Century.* NY: Knopf.

Ward, Lester F. 1902. *Dynamic Sociology.* Second edition. NY: Appleton.

———. 1907. *Pure Sociology.* Second edition. NY: Macmillan.

———. 1893. "Sociocracy." From *The Psychic Factors of Civilization* (Boston: Ginn & Co., 1893), pp. 315-331. As reprinted in *American Thought: Civil War to World War I* edited by Perry Miller (NY: Holt, Rinehart and Winston, 1954), pp. 306-320.

Wheatley, Margaret J. 1992. *Leadership and the New Science: Learning about Organization from an Orderly Universe.* San Francisco: Berrett-Koehler.

Weber, Max. 1947. *The Theory of Social and Economic Organization.* London: Free Press of Glencoe; Collier-Macmillan.

Weiner, Norbert. 1948. *Cybernetics; or Control and Communications in the Animal and the Machine.* NY: Wiley.

———. 1954. *The Human Use of Human Beings: Cybernetics and Society.* Boston: Houghton Mifflin.

Whyte, William Foote, and Kathleen King Whyte. 1988. *Making Mondragon: The Growth and Dynamics of the Worker Cooperative Complex.* Cornell International Industrial and Labor Relations Reports, no. 14. Ithaca, NY: ILR Press.

Wilber, Ken. 1996. *A Brief History of Everything.* Boston: Shambhala.

————. 2000. *Integral Psychology: Consciousness, Spirit, Psychology, Therapy.* Boston: Shambhala.

Zuboff, Shoshana. 1988. *In the Age of the Smart Machine.* NY: Basic Books.

————, and James Maxmin. 2002. *The Support Economy: Why Corporations Are Failing Individuals and the Next Episode of Capitalism.* NY: Viking Penguin.

Index

CPSIA information can be obtained at www.ICGtesting.com
Printed in the USA
LVOW07s1506090813

347176LV00002B/6/A